YORK NOTES

General Editors: Professor A.N. Jeffares (*University of Stirling*) & Professor Suheil Bushrui (*American University of Beirut*)

William Shakespeare

MACBETH

Notes by Alasdair D.F. Macrae

M.A. (EDINBURGH) *Lecturer in English Studies University of Stirling*

**LONGMAN
YORK PRESS**

The illustrations of the Globe Theatre are from
The Globe Restored in Theatre: A Way of Seeing by
C. Walter Hodges, published by Oxford University Press.
© Oxford University Press

YORK PRESS
Immeuble Esseily, Place Riad Solh, Beirut.

LONGMAN GROUP LIMITED
Longman House, Burnt Mill, Harlow,
Essex, CM20 2JE England
and Associated companies throughout the world

© Librairie du Liban 1980

First published 1980
Third impression 1983
ISBN 0 582 78096 9

Printed in Hong Kong by
Sing Cheong Printing Co Ltd

Contents

Part 1

Introduction

The life of William Shakespeare

William Shakespeare was born at Stratford upon Avon in 1564. His mother, Mary, came from a family of prosperous farmers and his father, John, variously described as a tanner, glove-maker and dealer in grain and meat, rose in wealth and importance during the earlier years of Shakespeare's life to occupy the most prominent positions in Stratford. As Shakespeare advanced in his fortunes, his father appears to have dropped out of public life.

It is likely that Shakespeare, because he was the eldest son, received a reasonable education in the local school. There are few records available to tell us much about Shakespeare's early adult life or how he made his way into the world of the theatre. He married Ann Hathaway when he was eighteen and, with a family to support, he must have taken some job to earn his living, but the first reference to Shakespeare's involvement in the theatre occurs in 1592 when a rival dramatist, Robert Greene, attacked the actor Shakespeare for daring to write plays. By this time he had collaborated with other authors in writing some plays and his own narrative poems and plays were establishing him as a new figure in the literary life of London. Almost certainly Shakespeare had entered the theatres as an actor in the mid-1580s and over the next twenty years there are references to him as a competent actor at the same time as his fame as a writer was growing. In 1596 the Shakespeare family, in his father's name, but probably on the strength of Shakespeare's success, was granted a coat of arms, an acknowledgement of a rise in society, and in 1597 Shakespeare felt prosperous enough to buy one of the largest houses in his native Stratford.

We know that from 1594 Shakespeare was a member of the theatrical company called the Chamberlain's Men and we know that when the company moved into the Globe Theatre in 1599 Shakespeare was a part-owner of the project. On the accession of James I to the throne, Shakespeare's company renamed itself the King's Men and the company frequently played before the king. By this time, Shakespeare was widely acclaimed as the leading playwright of his age and his popularity and financial success continued till his death in 1616 when he was fifty-two.

The exact dating of particular plays is not usually possible but a mixture of internal and external evidence helps us to place his thirty-seven plays in a rough chronological order between about 1589 and 1613. In the early years Shakespeare naturally experimented with different subjects and different forms. From about 1594 to 1600 he extended his writing in comedy, history plays and tragedy with particular stress on the first two categories. The period from 1600 to 1608 is dominated by his famous tragedies and in his last phase Shakespeare concentrated on sweet-sad plays in which he attempted to reconcile disappointment and loss with faith.

The facts about Shakespeare's life offered above are all of a public sort; we have virtually no record—apart from his poems and plays—of Shakespeare as a private individual. Many scholars have tried to construct the private Shakespeare from the evidence offered in his work but this attempt has led to as many Shakespeares as there are readers. It has also been doubted that the man called William Shakespeare wrote the plays; surely, say these doubters, the author of such masterpieces could not have been brought up in provincial Stratford, surely he must have been a man of incomparably varied experience, widely travelled, deeply read in the literature of Greece and Rome. We are left, after reading the doubters and speculators, with the works themselves and we must make of them what we can.

Literary and theatrical background

The second half of the sixteenth century was a period of experiment in English literature and by the end of the century a new confidence and versatility were being shown by many writers, not only in drama but in poetry and prose. The movement of ideas commonly called the Renaissance arrived in Britain some time after continental Europe and particularly Italy had felt its effects. By the time the Renaissance reached Britain it had become mingled with the shift in religious thinking of the Reformation. The influx of fresh theories and models added to a strong national consciousness may help to explain why the period from 1570 to 1620 became undoubtedly one of the most prolific and exciting in English literature.

The development of printing processes meant not only that new books could be published and circulated more quickly and widely but, through the translation of famous books from abroad and the compilation of histories based on newly available sources, the past of Europe became accessible to anyone who could read. This most distinguished effort of translation culminated in 1611 in the Authorised (by King James) Version of the Bible which, alongside the works of Shakespeare, occupies a central position in English literature.

Both Shakespeare's plays and the translation of the Bible share an eloquence, range and that mixture of inevitability and surprise of language which many critics would agree is the mark of poetic genius. How did this language come about? Shakespeare did not invent it; the Bible was translated by what amounted to a committee. In the rapid growth in English society in the sixteenth century the language, while holding on to the vocabulary of particular trades, professions and local activities, imported or created a vast new vocabulary to deal with the material entering the culture of England. In political theory, scientific experiment, theology, new words were needed for new ideas.

The development in literature which had the most crucial importance in drama was the refinement of blank verse as the verse form of plays. This refinement helped dramatists to break up speeches, to individualise them and to present the give and take, the interruptions, the dialogue of characters and not just the delivery of set speeches.

In the schools of the time the central subject was rhetoric, which was concerned with the methods of persuasion available in the handling of language. Until the printed book became cheap and literacy spread throughout the population, a person's authority with others had much to do with his ability to speak well. The prime examples of this skill were exhibited in the Court and church pulpits. The drama as an area of literature developed, in the main, out of an attempt to make religious stories and the struggle between good and evil more vivid. These religious plays originally based on biblical stories were called moralities and when the authors gradually adapted and elaborated on the stories with more freedom, the gap between the Church and the plays grew till it became necessary for the groups of actors to find an acting place outside the Church. It seems that these groups of actors came to be professional players who toured about with their secular entertainment from place to place, or stage to stage. Thus, the Elizabethan theatre had deep roots in a long oral tradition and it took strength and vitality from this shared experience of the people. *Macbeth* with all its artistry and complex structure dealt with themes of contemporary immediacy in a language and style readily accessible to its audience.

In London there were various sites favoured by the acting groups but it was not till 1576 that a permanent theatre building was erected on the edge of London. By the 1590s there were three such theatres in London and the pattern of the buildings was set for some years to come. The shape derived from the courtyards where plays had been acted and the basic plan of a stage, about fourteen metres wide by nine metres deep, projecting into the audience, was common to them all. At the back of the stage was a projecting balcony which could be used in scenes requiring differences in heights such as the battlements of a castle or the upper windows of a house. In the centre of the stage was a trap door through which characters could make sudden entrances or exits. A character could arrive on stage by swinging down from the balcony, emerging from below or coming through the doors at the back of the stage. Across the space under the balcony a curtain was hung

THE GLOBE PLAYHOUSE

The theatre, originally built by James Burbage in 1576, was made of wood (Burbage had been trained as a carpenter). It was situated to the north of the River Thames on Shoreditch in Finsbury Fields. There was trouble with the lease of the land, and so the theatre was dismantled in 1598, and reconstructed 'in an other forme' on the south side of the Thames as the Globe. Its sign is thought to have been a figure of the Greek hero Hercules carrying the globe. It was built in six months, its galleries being roofed with thatch. This caught fire in 1613 when some smouldering wadding, from a cannon used in a performance of Shakespeare's *Henry VIII*, lodged in it. The theatre was burnt down, and when it was rebuilt again on the old foundations, the galleries were roofed with tiles.

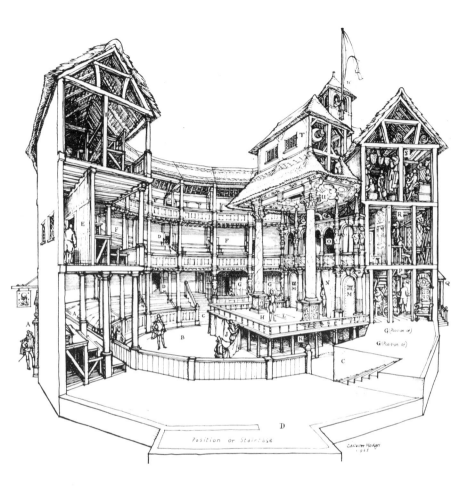

A CONJECTURAL RECONSTRUCTION OF THE INTERIOR OF THE GLOBE PLAYHOUSE

AA Main entrance
 B The Yard
CC Entrances to lowest gallery
 D Entrance to staircase and upper galleries
 E Corridor serving the different sections of the middle gallery
 F Middle gallery ('Twopenny Rooms')
 G 'Gentlemen's Rooms' or Lords' Rooms'
 H The stage
 J The hanging being put up round the stage
 K The 'Hell' under the stage
 L The stage trap, leading down to the Hell
MM Stage doors

N Curtained 'place behind the stage'
O Gallery above the stage, used as required sometimes by musicians, sometimes by spectators, and often as part of the play
P Back-stage area (the tiring-house)
Q Tiring-house door
R Dressing-rooms
S Wardrobe and storage
T The hut housing the machine for lowering enthroned gods, etc., to the stage
U The 'Heavens'
W Hoisting the playhouse flag

and there actors could change their costumes or wait for their next appearance. There is some evidence that this space could also be used as part of the acting area, particularly useful for scenes of surprise and intrigue. Sound effects and music could come also from both above or below. The audience were never far from the action and about 2,500 people from all classes of society could sit in tiers or stand in the pit (the ground) around the stage. These public theatres were open to the sky and if the weather was wet the performance would be postponed. No artificial light was needed and the scenery was simple; explanations about the time of day, location and period of the play were announced to the audience or written into the opening of scenes. Costume could be elaborate but was not in any way strictly in period according to our modern knowledge. Much emphasis must have been put on a clear and enunciated delivery of the lines and, although there is evidence of some spectacularly acrobatic acting, probably by present day conventions the acting was relatively static. As the theatres developed, as the standard of writing improved, so too did the professionalism of the actors. By the end of his writing career, Shakespeare could make demands of subtlety and restraint on the actors in his plays. Hamlet's advice to the Players (see *Hamlet* III.2) can be taken as applying to actors of the time. Richard Burbage was the main actor of tragic roles; Will Kemp and later Robert Armin were the celebrated clown-actors in Shakespeare's company. Female actors were forbidden by law and we have to imagine such characters as Desdemona in *Othello* and Lady Macbeth as played by boys.

The theatres described in the above paragraph were known as 'public' theatres; there were also 'private' theatres in the houses of wealthy people where official censorship, political or moral, could not easily be applied. In these indoor theatres lighting was by candles and it is an interesting possibility that *Macbeth* with its emphasis on darkness may have been devised for such a theatre.

Relevant ideas

Each society has some idea of order and is frightened of certain forces which seem, to that society, to threaten this order. In Shakespeare's England the order came to be seen as very precarious; almost every aspect of society was confronted with new and often frightening questions. Up till Shakespeare's lifetime and embodied in the strong personality of Queen Elizabeth the central and God-given position of the monarch was generally accepted. With the rise of radical Protestant thinking which had already usurped the power of the Pope, the formulation of new unscrupulous political theories particularly associated with Machiavelli, and the shift in real power from aristocratic titles and names to monetary capital in the hands of a merchant class, the framework of social order became open to the possibility of drastic change. A new spirit of experimental science was about which asked people to read the Bible for themselves, test laws on their own consciences, examine the evidence, not accept simply because a king or a priest stated some doctrine.

From medieval times European theology, philosophical and what we should now call social theory, had been concerned to construct a system which would show people how God, the Christian God, had arranged the world of His creation. In this perfect arrangement there could be no gaps, omissions or oddities. God had given men reason to allow them to see how His scheme operated. The whole of the created world came to be considered as a series of related categories or the links in a Great Chain of Being with God at the top and inanimate matter at the bottom. Man, possessed of both spirit and body, occupied a crucial link in this chain. In a similar way, the basis of all creation rested on the four elements, earth, air, fire, and water, each with its characteristic quality, or humour, (melancholy, sanguine, choleric and phlegmatic, respectively) and each man was a balance or imbalance of these elements.

This order of creation was present also in man's social world and similar gradations were traced in society from the monarch down to the least of his subjects. Furthermore, the interrelationship between the macrocosm (big world) of the universe and the microcosm (little world) of man was there for the individual person to witness. The circuits of the stars and planets, the changes in the natural world around him, were in no way irrelevant to man's behaviour but were in close sympathetic *rapport* with human actions. (See *Macbeth*, II.3.51–8 and III.4.121–5 for examples of the importance of this relationship between the macrocosm and microcosm). The law of Nature was given to all by God and conscience is the faculty by which individual man acknowledges this law. The crime of murder was a crime against this law of Nature and regicide (the murder of a king) was the murder of God's appointed leader.

Towards the end of Queen Elizabeth's reign in England (she ruled from 1558 to 1603) there were many rumours of rebellion and intrigue. Although Elizabeth had a stronger, more centralist government than any English ruler before her, this position was established at a considerable expense in the freedom of her subjects. The state-approved religion of Protestantism was constantly in danger of attack from inside and outside England, from both extremist Protestants, the Presbyterians, and Roman Catholics who manoeuvred in secret to have Elizabeth deposed and a brand of religion more favourable to them imposed. In 1587, Mary Queen of Scots, the main Roman Catholic contender for the throne, was executed by Elizabeth and in the following year the Spanish Armada, sent to depose Protestantism, was defeated by a mixture of luck and heroism. Every year men were arrested, executed, new plots were suspected, intrigues with foreign governments were detected and the rule of Elizabeth came to its end with the problems of political and religious stability~still unresolved. The Tudor line was at an end and Elizabeth's will alone could not prevent the throne from passing to the Stuarts.

The easiest way to attack a political rival was to accuse him of treachery and the easiest way to prove his treachery was to link him with one of the proscribed religious groups. In 1605 James dealt with some troublesome rivals by claiming to have detected a Catholic plot to blow up the Parliament. In Scotland, even more than in England at the time, political troublemakers were accused of witchcraft and heresy. James himself was an authority on witchcraft and the London edition of his *Daemonology* was published in 1603, the year of his accession to the throne of Great Britain. Certainly most people believed in the existence and power of witches, devils and ghosts and the religiously orthodox stressed that the Devil could take many shapes. According to the teaching of the Church, Heaven and Hell were actual places and the central teaching of Christianity was the sinful (fallen) nature of man and the necessity of a sense of guilt to bring the sinner to accept the salvation from sinfulness offered by Christ. The reason of man was not foolproof and the Church urged the faithful to be on their guard against any suggestion of communication with the Devil. At the opening of *Hamlet* genuine doubts concerning the authenticity of Hamlet's father's ghost are apparent and in Act I, Scene 3 of *Macbeth* similar fears are expressed by Banquo (the ancestor, according to legend, of King James) concerning the Witches:

> *Were such things here as we do speak about?*
> *Or have we eaten on the insane root*
> *That takes the reason prisoner?*
>
> (lines 82–84)

and

> *And oftentimes, to win us to our harm,*
> *The instruments of darkness tell us truths;*
> *Win us with honest trifles, to betray's*
> *In deepest consequence*
>
> (lines 122–125)

Mutability

In medieval writings one of the predominant concerns was with mutability or change, the fickleness and frailty of human life, the body always weakened by time, the vanity of human achievement. During the Renaissance increasing prestige came to be attached to individual prowess, to the attempt of one man to challenge mutability, to assert his human quality against change and adversity. It mattered little whether the effort took a religious way or a scholarly turn, like Erasmus, or an artistic direction, like Michelangelo (who died in the year of Shakespeare's birth), or a military mould, or a mixture of them all like Lorenzo (the Magnificent) de Medici—what mattered was the daring, the ambition of the effort. As the focus of scientific enquiry sharpened during the sixteenth century the immutability of absolute values and even the heavens, the macrocosm, came into question. The exploration of the New World, starting with the discovery of America in 1492 by Columbus, and of the shores of Africa, the degree of culture and learning revealed in the world of Islam from the time of the Crusades, the newly published knowledge of Greek and Roman civilisation, suggested that Western Europe was rather parochial and that there might be other ways of seeing the world and how it operated. In the same year as Shakespeare, Galileo Galilei was born and his scientific experiments, even if they were condemned by the Catholic Church, added to the growing weight of evidence that the medieval cosmology could not be maintained for much longer. If the earth was no longer the centre of the universe, if stars beyond stars had their own galaxies, if the biblical statement that the sun goes round the earth was wrong, where did this shift in conception leave man? If even the stars moved and died—and new stars appeared and disappeared thrice in Shakespeare's lifetime—if plague, war, rebellion, cruelty were the other face of Nature, what could man rely on? What was not subject to mutability? Shakespeare in his *Sonnets* asserts the value of human love and the durability of his art against the corrosion of time, but part of the charm and poignancy of these poems lies in our awareness of how fragile such an assertion is.

A note on the text

Macbeth was first published in 1623 in what is known as the First Folio, a collection of all but one (*Pericles*) of Shakespeare's plays made by John Heminges and Henry Condell who had known and acted with Shakespeare for twenty years. The text of *Macbeth* in the First Folio is very close to what we read in a modern edition of the play. However, the text of a Shakespeare play as we read it now is the result of careful work by many editors in the intervening years. Even in the case of *Macbeth*, not a difficult play editorially compared with some, editors have to make choices. For example, in the Folio Act I, Scene 7, Macbeth says to Lady Macbeth

> *I dare do all that may become a man,*
> *Who dares no more, is none*
>   (lines 46–47)

An editor over two hundred and fifty years ago suggested that 'do' makes easier sense than 'no' in line 47 and his suggestion has been accepted generally ever since. Some editors have doubted the genuineness of certain scenes, in particular the Porter Scene in Act II, Scene 3 and some of the Witches' appearances. The spelling, stage directions and line and even scene divisions are not always the same from one edition to another.

We know for certain that *Macbeth* was performed in 1611 because a very full eye-witness account survives. All the evidence available to us suggests that *Macbeth* was first performed in 1606, possibly in front of King James himself. The play was seriously altered in 1663 to bring it more into line with the taste of the period and this rather operatic version with songs and dances survived into the nineteenth century.

In modern times the play has been adapted and used in many guises. Among the many film versions, an American gangster feud has been one setting, a Japanese forest heavy with symbolism has been another. Most of the famous actors and actresses of the modern theatre have tested themselves in the exacting parts of Macbeth and Lady Macbeth.

Part 2

Summaries
of MACBETH

Act I Scene 1

Three Witches are gathered in an open place in a thunder storm. They agree to reassemble on the moorland before sunset to meet Macbeth.

COMMENTARY: The opening scene of a play is particularly important in establishing a mood or atmosphere in which the main action of the play will be seen by the audience. The scene is set in 'an open place', a place removed from the ordinary business of men and the usual social rules. The weather is extravagant and hostile to men, the 'fog and filthy air' suggesting unusual darkness and unhealthiness. The conversation of the Witches is again removed from the interchange of ordinary men; the use of rhyme is a feature of the Witches' speech and throughout the play it intensifies a sense of incantation, of magical charms. In line 4, 'When the battle's lost and won' and line 9, 'Fair is foul, and foul is fair' a curious paradox is offered. How can a battle be lost *and* won? How can fair be foul? What are opposites for us seem to be interchangeable for the Witches. And there is the appearance of the Witches themselves, traditionally ugly, barely human, often taking the shape of animals like cats and toads. Every detail of the short opening scene urges our imagination to sense a confusion of the usual human order, a reverse of human values, a world of darkness and foulness, a sinister challenge to ordinary goodness. And in the middle of the scene comes the startling line 'There to meet with Macbeth.' What can Macbeth, whose name gives the play its title, have to do with these abnormal, distasteful creatures? How does he fit in to their plans? They seem to know of the outcome of the battle before the battle is over.

NOTES AND GLOSSARY

hurly-burly: turmoil, confusion

Grey-Malkin: grey cat

Padock: toad (Cats and toads were the animals most commonly associated with witches and it was thought that witches could adopt the shapes or voices of these animals.)

Anon: at once

Act I Scene 2

Duncan, King of Scotland, with his two sons, Malcolm and Donalbain, and others is in an army camp receiving reports of the battles fought against him by an alliance of Sweno, King of Norway, Macdonwald, Lord of the Western Isles of Scotland, and the Thane of Cawdor who has proved disloyal to King Duncan. The reports direct from the fields of battle all stress the heroism of Macbeth, one of Duncan's generals, in ensuring the victory of the King's cause. Duncan, in gratitude for the victory, announces that Macbeth is to be given the title of Thane of Cawdor and the treacherous Cawdor is to be executed immediately.

COMMENTARY: The military alarum (sound of trumpets) is in contrast to the thunder and lightning of the first scene and the play shifts from the wild world of the Witches to the place where the royal authority is demonstrated. The focus of our attention in this scene is on Macbeth and on his virtues as a loyal soldier to King Duncan. The battle is given a size and an importance which magnify the qualities of Macbeth. Duncan has nothing but praise for the heroic deed of Macbeth. Our curiosity and anticipation are aroused to meet this mighty champion so praised by all who have seen him. But our memories still hold the mention of his name by the Witches and the final line of the scene reminds us of line 4 in Scene 1 and this connexion is consolidated in Scene 3.

NOTES AND GLOSSARY

newest state:	latest news
broil:	struggle
choke their art:	make it impossible for either to swim
for to ... upon him:	because, for that purpose, the innumerable nasty qualities (or people) crowd and grow on him like vermin
kerns and galloglasses:	lightly armed soldiers and heavily armed soldiers
showed... whore:	appeared to favour Macdonwald but, like a prostitute, prove unreliable
all's too weak:	all his efforts were inadequate
valour's minion:	the favourite of bravery (that is, Macbeth)
which:	who
unseamed ... chops:	split Macdonwald from his navel to his jaws
cousin:	(a common term of endearment in Elizabethan English but Macbeth was Duncan's cousin in the modern sense)

as . . . reflection:	just as when the sun is bright too early (and the subsequent day is stormy and disappointing)
spring:	source, early situation
skipping:	light-footed
trust their heels:	rely on flight
surveying vantage:	sensing an opportunity
furbished:	polished or provided
say sooth:	speak truthfully
overcharged . . . cracks:	loaded with double charges of explosive
except:	unless
reeking:	smoking, steaming (compare line 18)
memorize another Golgotha:	making the place as famous for slaughter as Golgotha (Hebrew word meaning place of the skulls), the site of Calvary where Christ was crucified
smack of:	indicate
Thane:	title of nobility in Scotland
Norweyan:	Norwegian, Viking
flout:	wave in defiance
fan . . . cold:	make the people cold with fear
Norway:	the King of Norway
Bellona:	Roman goddess of war
lapped in proof:	dressed in tested armour
confronted . . . self-comparisons:	faced him as an equal
point:	sword
lavish:	insolent
composition:	terms of peace
disbursed:	paid
Saint Colm's Inch:	Island of Inchcolm near Edinburgh
dollars:	coins (not actually in existence at the time of Macbeth)
bosom:	closest, dearest
present:	immediate

Act I Scene 3

The Witches recount the dreadful things they can do to men. As Macbeth and Banquo enter on their way home from their victory, the Witches prepare themselves with a charm. When challenged by the generals, the Witches greet Macbeth as Thane of Glamis, Thane of Cawdor and King to be, and Banquo is told that he will produce heirs who will become kings. The Witches disappear just before Ross and Angus arrive to announce that the King has conferred on Macbeth the title of Thane of Cawdor. Macbeth speculates to himself on what the future may hold for him and proposes to Banquo that they find time later to discuss the strange happening.

COMMENTARY: In the first two scenes of the play the world of the Witches has been separated from the world of men. Now these two worlds are brought together. The Witches' conversation emphasises that their evil and vindictive will cannot be thwarted by men. Their curse on the sea-captain can be read as a prediction of Macbeth's career. The rhymed incantation of the Witches' speech is again obvious. Macbeth's first line in the play arrests us because it is so close to the manner of the Witches and we remember, consciously or not, the end of Scene 1. The Witches answer Macbeth rather than Banquo and his reaction to the greeting of the Witches is quite different from that of Banquo; Macbeth is perturbed and frightened: Banquo is calm and sceptical. The confirmation of Macbeth as Thane of Cawdor adds to the puzzlement of Macbeth and Banquo, who is concerned that men are easily tempted into sin by the 'instruments of darkness'. In his asides, Macbeth reveals a deeply disturbed mind; something in himself seems to have been echoed in the Witches' words and it is this exposure of his inner mind that gives him most concern. Furthermore, if the Witches have been proved right about the Thane of Cawdor, then the next stage may be inevitable. Or, does he have to act? In the first scene in which he appears, Macbeth reveals a strong power of imagination and even at this early stage he tries to deceive people (see lines 149–150).

NOTES AND GLOSSARY

Aroint thee:	get off!
rump-fed ronyon:	fat-bottomed slut
Tiger:	(there was an actual ship of this name which returned in 1606 after a bad voyage)
sieve:	(witches defied the laws of nature)
rat . . . tail:	(witches took the shape of animals but not the tail)
I'll do:	I'll deal with him
ports . . . card:	she controls all the winds and can cause them to blow from whichever unfavourable direction of the compass she chooses
penthouse lid:	eyelid (like a sloping roof)
forbid:	accursed
peak:	grow thinner
pine:	waste away

(

bark:	ship
Wierd:	(the old English word for Destiny)
posters:	fast travellers
wound up:	prepared, complete
is't called:	is it said to be
choppy:	rough and cut
fantastical:	imaginary
present grace:	(that is, Thane of Glamis)
prediction ... having:	(Thane of Cawdor)
royal hope:	(the throne of Scotland)
rapt:	entranced, spellbound
Sinell:	Macbeth's father
corporal:	bodily, material
insane root:	some narcotic plant
post:	messenger
earnest:	pledge
addition:	title
borrowed robes:	the garments (and qualities) of another person
line:	support
vantage:	opportunity
wrack:	destruction
capital:	most serious
behind:	still to come
home:	completely
enkindle:	encourage you to hope
consequence:	seriousness
swelling:	magnificent (the image is from the theatre)
soliciting:	offer, invitation
seated:	fixed
single state:	whole being
function:	the ability to act
surmise:	speculation
nothing ... not:	the future, the imagined has cancelled out the present, the actual
will have me:	intends me to be
my stir:	me doing anything
strange:	new
cleave ... mould:	fit the wearer
come ... day:	whatever is going to happen will happen whatever the day looks like
stay ... leisure:	await your convenience
favour:	pardon

wrought: troubled
you pains ... read them: (that is, in his memory)
at more ... it: later, when we have had time to consider the matter
free hearts: honest feelings

Act I Scene 4

In the palace at Forres Duncan hears his son, Malcolm, relate how the treacherous Cawdor has been executed. Macbeth enters and is warmly welcomed by the King. Banquo is also commended. Duncan announces that Malcolm is to be the heir to the throne and confers on him the title of Prince of Cumberland. When Duncan voices his intention to travel to Inverness (Macbeth's castle), Macbeth sets out to take the news to his wife and prepare a welcome for his King. Macbeth realises that the new Prince of Cumberland is an obstacle to his ambition and proposes to act quickly.

COMMENTARY: We are presented with a picture of royal order and justice. The portrait of the dying Cawdor as penitent and dignified is placed against the arrival of Macbeth. Duncan shows himself to be an innocent and trusting person and addresses Macbeth as 'worthiest cousin'. Macbeth answers Duncan's thanks and praise in an obedient but ornate manner. Notice the emphasis on 'service', 'loyalty', 'owe', 'your highness', 'duties', 'state', 'safe', 'love', 'honour'—all in half a dozen lines. Macbeth's words suggest a model of the loyal subject but already we know something of another side to Macbeth. Banquo thanks the King by merely completing the metaphor (of growing) used by Duncan. Shakespeare's choice of this moment for Duncan to namè his successor is very shrewd dramatically. Duncan's announcement forces Macbeth's mind further into his thoughts of the previous scene and when Duncan indicates that he will spend the night in Macbeth's castle we suspect hollowness and untrustworthiness in Macbeth's saying

> I'll be myself the harbinger, and make joyful
> The hearing of my wife with your approach.

In his aside Macbeth invokes darkness to hide his intentions and we think back to the 'instruments of darkness' of the previous scene. The stars which by Duncan are likened to 'signs of nobleness' (line 42), are extinguished at Macbeth's command (line 51).

NOTES AND GLOSSARY
flourish: fanfare (of trumpets)
in commission: authorised to conduct the execution
liege: lord

became him:	suited him, did him honour
that . . . studied:	who had learned a part (like an actor)
owed:	owned
careless:	worthless
there's no art . . . face:	there is no certain way of knowing a man's character from his face
proportion:	balance (as of money in a bank)
which do:	(that is, the duties do)
safe:	entirely
enfold:	embrace
wanton:	unrestrained
drops of sorrow:	tears (of joy)
establish our estate:	settle the succession (to the throne of Scotland)
unaccompanied invest:	exclusively apply to
bind . . . you:	put us deeper in your debt
the rest . . . you:	leisure is a burden if it is not employed to prepare for you .
harbinger:	messenger (originally an official sent ahead to arrange accommodation for the King)
wink at:	be blind to
let that be:	let that action be done
in . . . am fed:	I am filled by praising him
kinsman:	(Macbeth is Duncan's first cousin)

Act I Scene 5

In Inverness Castle Lady Macbeth is reading a letter sent to her by Macbeth after he had met the Witches but before he met Duncan. Lady Macbeth's mind immediately looks forward to the fulfilment of the Witches' prophecy but she feels that Macbeth is too mild to seize the throne. A messenger arrives with the news that Duncan plans to spend the night in the Castle and, by the time her husband enters, Lady Macbeth has already prepared her mind for the murder of Duncan. Macbeth wavers but Lady Macbeth's resolution is absolute.

COMMENTARY: There is no preparation of the audience for the character of Macbeth's wife. She appears in this scene as a ruthless, totally committed woman whose every effort is to strive for the greater glory of her husband. Macbeth's tendency to speculate and think round problems, a quality we noted in Scene 3, is seen by his wife as a crucial weakness. He does not lack ambition but he is squeamish about the methods to be used to achieve this ambition. The hardness necessary for an assassination must come from her. There is an element in Lady Macbeth's attitude strongly reminiscent of the Witches; she talks of pouring her spirits in Macbeth's ear like some potion to alter his character and she invokes the spirits of evil to defeminise her, to dehumanise her, and like Macbeth in the previous scene, she prays for darkness to hide her planned action. The chain of imperatives ('come', 'fill', etc) gives her speech a special urgency and determination. When Macbeth appears there is little trace of endearment from his wife. She sees him and forces him to see himself in terms of her plan for power. She addresses him as he had been addressed by the Witches in Scene 3 and there is a drastic brevity in her language: 'He that's coming must be provided for.' The arrival of the Messenger announcing Duncan's visit is a brilliant dramatic stroke. We know that Duncan is coming but what is so startling is the Messenger's arrival immediately after Lady Macbeth has voiced her plans. 'The King comes here tonight' is the anticipation of her dearest wish. Even Lady Macbeth falters—for a moment.

NOTES AND GLOSSARY

perfectest report: the best knowledge (either he has made enquiries about the Witches or his own experience has proved them right)

missives: messengers

deliver thee: report to you

dues of rejoicing; appropriate joy

milk of human kindness: gentleness of decent humanity

illness should attend it: necessary wickedness

what thou ... holily: what you would like passionately to have you would like to obtain by fair means

thou'dst have ... undone: you would like to have something (the crown) but it demands, 'You must do this' if you wish it, and you are more afraid to do this necessary job than eager to reverse it if it were actually done

hie: hasten

chastise ... tongue: correct or strengthen with my strong words

golden round: crown

metaphysical: supernatural

informed: sent word ahead

had the speed of him: came faster than he did

raven: bird announcing death

mortal: deadly

crown: top of her head

thick:	(so that pity cannot pass to her heart)
remorse:	compassion
compunctions . . . nature: natural feelings of pity	
fell:	dreadful
nor keep . . . it:	nor intervene between my intention and its fulfilment
for gall:	in exchange for sour vinegar
ministers:	evil spirits
sightless:	invisible
waite on nature's mischief: attend on the disasters and evil possible in the world	
pall:	wrap, hide as in a coffin cloth
dunnest:	darkest
hereafter:	of the future (the third prophecy)
ignorant:	unknowing
instant:	present
to beguile . . . time: to deceive people now appear as they expect to see you	
provided for:	dealt with (ironic way of saying killed)
dispatch:	care
look up clear:	appear cheerful
to alter . . . fear:	to show a disturbed face is a betrayal of troubled thoughts

Act I Scene 6

Duncan and his attendant lords arrive at Macbeth's castle. While they are admiring the peaceful location of the castle they are welcomed by Lady Macbeth and she and Duncan exchange greetings and compliments.

COMMENTARY: The emphasis of this scene, as in Scene 4, is on peace, trust and courtesy. After the passion and vicious emotions of Scene 5 we are presented with images of tranquillity and the words 'guest' and 'host' are repeated. Lady Macbeth appears as the perfect, sophisticated hostess but we remember her advice to her husband:

> *Look like the innocent flower*
> *But be the serpent under't.*

The calm light of evening comes before the darkness of the following scenes.

NOTES AND GLOSSARY

hautboys:	oboes
torches:	torchbearers
seat:	position
nimbly:	freshly
gentle:	calm
temple-haunting martlet:	the house martin likes to nest in the eaves of tall buildings like churches
approve:	prove
by his loved mansionry:	by building his nest here
jutty, frieze, buttress:	architectural features that stick out from the walls
coign of vantage:	suitable corner
pendent ... cradle:	hanging nest for breeding in
haunt:	frequent
the love ... trouble:	(he means that love can be burdensome in that it puts one in debt to the giver but it is, nonetheless, a great blessing)
single:	feeble
business:	service, effort
we rest your hermits:	we still pray for you
coursed:	chased
purveyor:	the official who went ahead of the King to arrange his food
holp:	helped
your servants ... your own:	(she means that all that belongs to Macbeth really belongs to the King and he can claim any of it at any time)
by your leave:	with your permission (he would kiss Lady Macbeth on the cheek)

Act I Scene 7

Macbeth has slipped out of the supper-room and is having second thoughts on the plan to murder Duncan. He is aware of the seriousness of his proposed crime as an act of treachery against an innocent guest. When Lady Macbeth finds him, Macbeth has decided to cancel the plan but his wife persuades him to change his mind. She outlines her tactics and Macbeth cannot but admire her resolution. He steels himself for the murder.

COMMENTARY: Macbeth's final words in Scene 5 were, 'We shall speak further'. His wavering then is continued in the present scene but when

Lady Macbeth joins him they do not conduct a real discussion: she tells him what is to be done. Macbeth allows himself to imagine the future beyond the murder in a way which Lady Macbeth forbids herself. His will is weakened by speculation; her will is strengthened by a concentration on the act of killing Duncan. It is the difference between Why? and How? Lady Macbeth's main argument is that her husband has to prove his manhood by acting decisively. Macbeth knows that there is another concept of Man (lines 46–7) but he is dominated by a woman prepared to renounce the essence of her femininity until his argument is reduced to the cowardly line, 'If we should fail?' Failure is not something that Lady Macbeth bothers to contemplate. In his final two speeches in the scene Macbeth adopts the manner of speaking of his wife and the echo of Lady Macbeth's earlier sentiments (see Scene 5, 61–4) in his last couplet is not accidental. We remember also the significant line of the Witches in Scene 1, 'Fair is foul, and foul is fair' and Macbeth's own 'So foul and fair a day I have not seen' (Scene 3, line 37) and we realise that the preparations are complete. We await the action.

NOTES AND GLOSSARY

sewer: the equivalent of a modern head waiter (originally he was the person who tested the food given to the King)

divers: various

if it were done: if the murder were finished and done with

trammel: catch together (like a net)

with his surcease success: what I want (success) by his death

the be-all and the end-all: all that is to be and what completes everything

bank and shoal: life like a sand bank in the sea of eternity

jump . . . come: risk the judgement of the after life

still: always

even-handed: impartial

commends: offers

ingredience: contents

chalice: drinking vessel (particularly in the Christian communion service)

strong both: both strong arguments

faculties: powers (as King)

clear: incorrupt

taking-off: departure, murder

naked new-born babe: (suggests compassion for the innocent and helpless)

striding the blast:	astride the storm (of protest)
cherubin:	angel
sightless curriers:	invisible winds
blow:	broadcast (or trumpet)
tears ... wind:	tears of pity shall outdo the wind of indignation
spur ... sides:	powerful or moral incentive to urge him, just like a horse approaching a jump, into the act of murder
vaulting:	soaring, aspiring
o'erleaps ... other:	jumps beyond its control and comes to grief over the jump
bought:	gained (by his deeds)
would:	should
newest gloss:	new and shining
green and pale:	(the effects of being drunk)
such:	as drunken boasting
ornament of life:	the crown
poor cat i' the adage:	(the cat in the proverb wanted to eat a fish but was not prepared to wet his feet in order to catch it)
prithee, peace:	I pray you, stop speaking
none:	not a man
break this enterprise:	voice this plan
did then adhere:	were convenient then
fitness:	suitability (of time and place)
screw ... sticking place:	tighten your courage like the string holding the arrow in a cross-bow which is ready for shooting
the rather:	certainly
chamberlains:	personal servants
wassail:	feasting
convince:	overpower
memory ... limbeck only:	memory, the guardian of reason, will be converted into a vapour (by alcohol) and the brain act as a distilling unit
drenched:	drunken
spongy:	filled with drink
quell:	murder
mettle:	spirit
received:	believed
bend ... agent:	strain (like a bow-string) every part of my being
mock the time:	deceive everyone

Act II Scene 1

It is after midnight and Banquo and Fleance, his son, are preparing to go to bed. Banquo feels some uneasiness but when Macbeth appears suddenly out of the darkness he converses politely and passes on Duncan's compliments to Macbeth and a diamond for Lady Macbeth. Macbeth advises Banquo to side with him in the future. Left on his own, Macbeth waits for the signal from his wife; his imagination conjures out of the air a dagger which he cannot grasp. He prepares his mind for the murder and the signal sounds.

COMMENTARY: Immediately before the murder we are presented with Banquo and Macbeth who have both gained military glory, promising prophecies from the Witches, and praise from the King. It would seem from lines 7–9 and line 20 that the meeting with the Witches has made a lasting impression on Banquo's mind and he is deeply disturbed by the workings of his subconscious mind in dreams. His trust rests on God and the help of his angels. Macbeth too has an imaginative flight in the scene but in his soliloquy he allies himself with witchcraft, murder and secrecy. The contrast with Banquo is carefully offered at this point. The 'summons' to sleep that Banquo feels in line 6 has become a summons 'to Heaven or to Hell' for Duncan according to Macbeth in the final line of the scene.

NOTES AND GLOSSARY

husbandry:	economy
their candles:	the stars of heaven
summons:	tiredness which calls him
powers:	the order of angels who protect man from devils
largess:	generous gifts
offices:	servants
shut up ... content:	gone to bed completely happy
our will ... wrought:	we were not able to be as hospitable as we should have wished
entreat to serve:	find the time
your kind'st leisure:	your convenience
cleave ... when 'tis:	side with me when the time comes
honour ... none:	(Macbeth seems to mean gain; Banquo means honesty)
bosom ... clear:	heart free from guilt and loyalty unspoilt
sensible to feeling:	able to be touched
heat-oppressèd:	fevered
palpable:	able to be touched

marshall'st:	indicate
dudgeon:	handle
gouts:	drops
informs:	creates shapes
half-world:	hemisphere
abuse:	deceive
Hecat:	goddess of witchcraft
offrings:	ceremonies, rituals
alarumed:	aroused
watch:	indication of time
Tarquin's ravishing strides:	Tarquin raped Lucretia in the night (see Shakespeare's poem *The Rape of Lucrece*)
prate:	tell
take ... the time:	broadcast the horror beyond this time
knell:	bell sounded to announce a death

Act II Scene 2

Lady Macbeth has drugged Duncan's servants and now, stimulated by wine, she awaits the completion of the murder and the return of her husband. Macbeth enters, almost out of his mind, unable to distance himself from the scene in Duncan's room. He is rebuked by his wife who, seizing control of the situation, finds that she has to take the daggers back because Macbeth has removed them and is incapable of returning to the scene of his crime. A sound of knocking is heard and Macbeth is led out by his wife to wash off the blood and change into his dressing-gown.

COMMENTARY: A scene of intense excitement where the suspense worked up by Lady Macbeth's vivid recounting of her preparations is heightened by her jumpiness and is not in any way relieved by the return of Macbeth with the news, 'I have done the deed'. Macbeth's state of mind verges on the hysterical and the extreme tension is communicated to us so that we are forced to participate in it by the abrupt changes of direction in the speech of the characters, the interruptions, the sudden noises, the questions, the exclamations. We are trapped in Macbeth's anguish and, like Lady Macbeth, we struggle for control. We see the bloody daggers in Macbeth's hands and, like the characters, we come to fear discovery—such is our involvement, our complicity in the murder. We feel that *we* cannot go back with the daggers, and, when the knocking repeatedly sounds, *we* are held in the hysteria of Macbeth and are grateful to be led off by the masterful Lady Macbeth.

NOTES AND GLOSSARY

quenched:	put them out (to sleep)
owl:	bird associated with death (as are crickets in line 15)
fatal bellman:	the man who rings the bell announcing the execution of a condemned criminal
stern'st:	most solemn
surfeited grooms:	drunken servants
charge:	duty
possets:	bed-time drinks
addressed:	prepared
hangman:	executioner
knits . . . sleave:	arranges the tangled threads
second course:	the most nourishing course of a meal
unbend:	loosen
witness:	evidence
infirm:	weak
as pictures:	look the same
gild . . . guilt:	cover with golden blood (a play on words)
how is't:	what is wrong
Neptune:	Roman god of the sea
rather:	instead
multitudinous:	extensive
incarnadine:	turn red
one:	totally
your . . . unattended:	your firmness of mind has deserted you
watchers:	awake
poorly:	helplessly

Act II Scene 3

As the knocking increases the Porter, still drunk, organises himself to open the gate and, eventually, he lets Macduff and Lennox enter. Macbeth appears apparently wakened by the noise. When Macduff who has gone to waken the King returns with the news of his murder and raises the alarm, Macbeth and Lennox go to investigate. Lady Macbeth enters followed by Banquo and, while the news is discussed, Macbeth relates how he killed the blood-covered servants in his fury. Lady Macbeth faints and in the ensuing confusion Malcolm and Donalbain decide to slip away because they fear for their lives. Banquo proposes a general meeting to discuss the situation and the others agree.

COMMENTARY: The tension of the previous scene is maintained by the knocking and by our feeling that the discovery of the murder is merely being delayed by the rambling talk. The horror of the murder is intensified by the coarse vulgarity of the Porter; he seems, in his comic bad taste to be a gruesome attempt to cover-up the truth. He does, however, when we examine his words more carefully (see commentary, page 57), give a contemporary and a universal significance to Macbeth's crime. Lennox's observations develop this wider significance. Also, the confused quality of the Porter's speech and our uncertainty as to what is happening suggest a general confusion which, in fact, occupies the rest of the scene. Macbeth and Lady Macbeth's actions and words are a mixture of the extravagant and plausible. It is interesting to compare Macbeth's words in lines 88–93 with his speech in V.5.17–28, Banquo, more than Macbeth, proves himself the master of the situation and his speech near the end of the scene is judicious, firm and clear-spoken. The flight of Malcolm and Donalbain is an intimation of the distrust and moral confusion soon to be seen as characteristic of Macbeth's behaviour as king.

NOTES AND GLOSSARY

old:	plenty (of work)
Belzebub:	the devil
come in time (time-server in some editions): come in good time (or come in, you opportunist)
napkins enow:	plenty of handkerchiefs
equivocator:	one who tampers with the truth to suit his argument (The Catholic Jesuits involved in the plot against King James in 1605 were notorious for their equivocations)
stealing . . . hose:	cheating by using less material in the trousers than he claimed
roast your goose:	heat your tailor's iron (or it may mean cure your venereal disease)
primrose . . . bonfire:	the seductive, pleasurable way to hell
second cock:	3 o'clock in the morning
provoker:	encourager
lechery . . . leaves him: the Porter is claiming here that alcohol arouses a man sexually but weakens his ability at the same time
gave . . . the lie:	knocked you down
made a shift:	managed
cast:	throw him off, vomit

timely:	early
physics:	counteracts
limited:	appointed
service:	duty
dire combustion:	impending disasters
to the woeful time:	for the time of distress
obscure bird:	owl
confusion:	destruction
the Lord's anointed temple:	the body and the King
Gorgon:	(anyone who looked at this mythical monster was turned to stone)
downy:	gentle
counterfeit:	imitation
the Great Doom's image:	a picture of the Final Judgement Day
countenance:	face
serious:	worthwhile
lees:	dregs of wine
vault:	wine cellar, the arch of the sky
amiss:	wrong
badged:	marked
expedition:	haste
pauser:	what should make one hesitate
laced:	criss-crossed
wasteful:	destructive
unmannerly breeched:	disgustingly covered
that most ... for ours:	who are most involved in this business
auger-hole:	a tiny, unsuspected hole
brewed:	matured
upon the foot of motion:	able to do anything
naked frailties:	underclad bodies (but this also implies human feelings)
scruples:	doubts
undivulged pretence:	unrevealed aims
manly readiness:	suitable clothes (or prepared as men)
consort:	gather
office:	duty
the near:	the nearer
shaft:	arrow
lighted:	landed finally
aim:	man who aims
dainty:	particular
There's ... steals itself:	it is justified (theft) to steal away

Act II Scene 4

Ross and an Old Man discuss the extraordinary confusion in the natural world and draw a parallel between it and the unnatural human acts of the night. Macduff enters and reports that suspicion for the responsibility of the murder rests on the departed Malcolm and Donalbain. Macbeth has gone to be crowned in Scone.

COMMENTARY: We receive a view of the incident from people not directly concerned in it. The Old Man, significantly given the biblical span of life, is representative of the common man and the murder of Duncan is made more horrific by its uniqueness in his experience. The turbulence in the macrocosm, the reversals of natural law, reflect the enormity of Macbeth's crime. The second half of the scene is mainly an informative link between the murder and subsequent developments in the play but the scene ends with a human and Christian hope that the traditional values will be restored.

NOTES AND GLOSSARY

trifled former knowings:	made earlier experience seem trifling
heavens ... act ... stage:	(all have a theatrical sense)
travelling lamp:	sun
predominance:	supremacy (of the power of darkness)
towering ... place:	soaring to the highest point of her flight
mousing:	(usually content to) hunt mice
minions:	darlings, best
flung out:	lashed out
pretend:	hope for
suborned:	paid to commit a crime
thriftless:	wasteful
ravin up:	ravenously devour
means:	support, basis
named:	chosen
Scone:	place where Scottish kings were crowned
invested:	crowned as king
Colmekill:	Iona, a holy island, where Scottish kings were buried
Fife:	Macduff's territory
adieu:	(French for) good-bye
lest ... new:	(it may be that the new regime will be less comfortable to us)
benison:	blessing
good ... foes:	see the best in people (a reference to the peacemakers of the Bible)

Act III Scene 1

Macbeth has settled into the Royal Palace at Forres. Banquo has serious suspicions about how the Witches' prophecies for Macbeth have been fulfilled but he and, it turns out, Macbeth, remember the Witches' prediction for his descendants. Publicly, Banquo and Macbeth are polite and diplomatic but when Banquo leaves to go riding, Macbeth, aware of the threat posed by Banquo's qualities, arranges for his murder and the murder of Fleance by two villains whose minds he turns against Banquo.

COMMENTARY: We see Macbeth in this scene as the established King but his mind is not secure. We hear Banquo's thoughts of Macbeth before we hear the King's own thoughts and Shakespeare has arranged the thoughts in parallel so that they refer forward and back to each other. But Banquo says nothing of Macbeth's qualities as a king or even as a man, whereas Macbeth presents a generous analysis of Banquo's character. Both men seem to be obsessed by the predictions of the Witches concerning the descendants of Banquo. Macbeth, however, thinks that he can negate the prediction by killing Banquo and Fleance even though the same prophets have been proved correct in his own case. Notice the casual skill with which Macbeth ascertains Banquo's movements and the care he takes, so as to avoid any suspicion, to mention repeatedly the importance he places on Banquo's presence at the special supper in the evening and at the meeting the following day. It seems curious that Shakespeare devotes so much time, about seventy lines, to Macbeth's meeting with the two Murderers. The sorting-out and manipulation of other people are marks of the tyrant. 'To be thus is nothing, but to be safely thus', he says while waiting for the Murderers and his elaborate briefing of them is an attempt to persuade himself of how foolproof his plan is. He, paradoxically, appeals to them as men.

NOTES AND GLOSSARY
stand ... posterity: continue in your family
sennet: a set of notes played on the trumpet
all-thing: totally
solemn: ceremonious
still: always
grave and prosperous: weighty and profitable
invention: lies
craving us jointly: demanding us both
our time ... upon us: it is time for us to go

while:	till
thus:	(king)
would:	must
dauntless temper:	fearless quality
genius is rebuked:	guardian spirit is held down
chid:	challenged
sceptre:	(the symbol of the King)
unlineal:	outside my family
issue:	descendants
filed:	defiled, corrupted
rancours ... peace:	bitterness in my calm of mind
eternal jewel:	soul
enemy:	Devil
list:	struggle (tournament)
champion ... utterance:	fight me to the death
made good:	explained
passed in probation:	showed the proof
borne in hand:	deceived
crossed:	tricked
half ... crazed:	a simpleton
so gospelled:	(such Christians)
yours:	your families
hounds, etc:	different breeds of dogs
clept:	called
valued file:	list showing the qualities and value
particular addition:	individual description (unlike the bill and catalogue)
file ... rank:	the positions of men in an army; file suggests more quality
grapples:	holds you tight
his:	Banquo's
tugged with:	pulled about by
in such bloody distance:	of such a fatal closeness
near'st of life:	very being
avouch:	justify
for:	because of
wail:	must lament
sundry:	various
perfect spy:	exact information
something:	some distance
thought:	bearing in mind
clearness:	clean reputation

rubs nor botches:	flaws or mistakes
material:	important
embrace:	share
resolve:	make your plan
straight:	immediately

Act III Scene 2

Lady Macbeth realises that the satisfaction she and Macbeth had sought has not been achieved. She tries to enter into her husband's obsessive involvement while, at the same time, trying to reassure him and urge him to cheerfulness. Macbeth is tormented, his thoughts are fixed on Banquo. He hints at black deeds to come.

COMMENTARY: A pathetic development in the relationship of Macbeth and Lady Macbeth is revealed. They feel similarly about the situation (compare lines 4–7 and 19–22) but are unable to share their thoughts with each other and, by now, Macbeth has detached himself from his reliance on his wife and pursues his own course. It is remarkable that in the middle of this scene he can ask his wife to act pleasantly to Banquo when we know that Banquo, on his orders, will never return. His brutalised nature is evident in the cool 'Be innocent of the knowledge, dearest chuck, Till thou applaud the deed.' Significantly, he invokes the same powers of darkness and witchcraft as he had called on earlier in Act II, Scene 1, lines 51–60.

NOTES AND GLOSSARY

had:	gained
doubtful:	apprehensive, insecure
sorriest:	most miserable
using:	(as companions)
without regard:	out of thought
scorched:	slashed
close:	recover
poor malice:	weak attack
former tooth:	still poisonous fangs
frame . . . disjoint:	the whole universe break apart
both . . . worlds:	heaven and earth
ere:	before
ecstasy:	delirium
fitful:	restless
levy:	troops

sleek o'er:	smooth
jovial:	Jove-like (the god of festivity)
remembrance:	reminder
present him eminence:	honour him
unsafe ... streams:	while we are unsafe we must give a clean look to our honour by using streams of flattery
vizards:	masks
nature's ... eterne	(they are made in God's image but are not immortal)
jocund:	joyful
cloistered:	round cloisters of churches, or dark
shard-born:	born in dung, or carried on its scaly wings
yawning peal:	call to sleep
note:	significance
chuck:	chick (term of endearment)
seeling:	blinding (as is done to a hawk's eyelids)
scarf:	blindfold
bond:	the moral (biblical) law which forbids killing
pale:	anxious
thickens:	dims
rooky:	full of rooks
ill:	evil, worse

Act III Scene 3

Some distance from the Palace, a third Murderer, sent by Macbeth, joins the two waiting to ambush Banquo and Fleance. In the gathering darkness they kill Banquo but Fleance escapes.

COMMENTARY: Macbeth cannot trust the two Murderers and sends one of his men to make sure the job is done. When Fleance escapes Macbeth's scheme has more than failed; he has increased suspicions of his villainy and the prophecy of the Witches, which he had hoped to cancel, is still there to torment him. Banquo himself was not the real danger and Macbeth's already overwhelmed conscience is further pressed under the weight of a murder he knows to be indefensible.

NOTES AND GLOSSARY

He ... mistrust:	there is no reason for us to distrust him (the newcomer)
offices:	instructions
to ... just:	just as we were directed

lated:	belated
apace:	quickly
timely:	welcome
within . . . expectation:	on the list of expected guests
about:	the long way round (to the stables)
way:	right thing to do
best . . . affair:	the more important part of the job, or the larger part of the reward

Act III Scene 4

As Macbeth and Lady Macbeth are welcoming the guests to the feast, one of the Murderers arrives and tells Macbeth of the death of Banquo and the escape of Fleance. Macbeth turns back to the table and comments on Banquo's absence. Banquo's ghost enters and occupies Macbeth's place; he is visible only to Macbeth. Lady Macbeth tries to calm her husband and keep control of the situation but after the ghost has disappeared and Macbeth seems to be recovering, suddenly, again on Macbeth's mentioning his name, Banquo's ghost reappears and Macbeth is rendered helpless. After the ghost has gone for the second time, Lady Macbeth brings the feast to a hurried end. Macbeth informs Lady Macbeth that he intends to visit the Witches and press on with eliminating all opposition.

COMMENTARY: This, the halfway scene in the play, is a central scene in the analysis of Macbeth's career in crime. The newly established King holds a lavish feast to show his authority and at the beginning of the scene we have the ceremony of guests and hosts and civilised order interrupted by the sly appearance of Macbeth's hired killer. The facade of decency has a murderous heart and the appearance of Banquo's ghost is the harsh reminder of Macbeth's wickedness. The ghost is the externalised form of Macbeth's guilt and fear of discovery, invisible to the others but a terrifying reality to Macbeth himself. His wife loyally and resourcefully tries to protect him and shake him out of his obsession but, as she says, Macbeth is 'quite unmanned in folly'. Macbeth, a man celebrated for his courage in battle, cringes before the creation of his troubled conscience. When the ghost and the guests have gone, Macbeth's mind is not restored to calmness or repentance or even full trust in his wife. He can see no way out of his dilemma but by crushing everyone around him who questions his will. Fate, including the Witches, must be bullied into obedience. This is the final appearance of a sane Lady Macbeth. Her iron self-control, loyalty to her husband, organising skill, apparent callousness—all evident in this scene—are qualities she possesses but, as we shall see, she has paid dearly for them.

NOTES AND GLOSSARY

degrees:	places at table (according to importance)
at first and last:	from beginning to end
state:	special chair of state
in best:	at the most suitable
require:	request
encounter:	answer
sides:	(of the table)
be large in mirth:	enjoy yourselves
the nonpareil:	without equal
whole:	solid
founded:	secure
broad and general:	free and unconfined
casing:	surrounding
cabined, etc.:	imprisoned
saucy:	molesting
trenched:	cut deep
worm:	young serpent
ourselves:	each other
cheer:	welcome, or a toast
the feast ... without it:	unless repeated welcomes are given a feast is like a paid-for meal; food itself is better at home but outside one expects more ceremony to make the meal worthwhile
honour roofed:	all the nobility present
graced:	gracious
mischance:	misfortune
moves:	disturbs
gory locks:	blood covered hair
upon a though:	in a moment
note:	make a fuss
passion:	fit
proper stuff!:	nonsense
flaws:	outbursts
grandam:	grandmother
if charnel houses ... kites:	if tombs cannot hold down the dead we will need to have them eaten by birds of prey
purged ... weal:	civilised society
mortal murthers:	fatal wounds

crowns:	heads
lack:	miss
thirst:	wish to drink
all to all:	everyone toast everyone
duties:	homage
pledge:	the toast
avaunt!:	away!
speculation:	intelligence
Hyrcan:	(near the Caspian Sea)
inhabit:	have in me
protest:	accuse
baby:	doll
admired:	amazing
overcome:	come over
strange . . . owe:	wonder about my own nature
order:	(of rank)
it will have:	murder demands
augurs:	prophecies
relations:	connections in nature
maggot-pies, etc:	(birds)
man of blood:	murderer
how say'st thou:	what do you say to the fact
denies his person:	refuses his presence
feed:	bribed
betimes:	very early
bent:	determined
causes:	considerations
may be scanned:	can be examined
season:	preservative, or freshening
my . . . use:	my strange delusion is the result of a beginner's fear, one who needs more experience
deed:	crimes

Act III Scene 5

On the heath, Hecat, the ruler of all witches, is angry that she has not been consulted about the previous dealings with Macbeth. She tells them to prepare for a meeting with him in the morning and she predicts his downfall.

COMMENTARY: Many scholars doubt whether this scene was written by Shakespeare but in its imagery and attitude to Macbeth it fits easily into the rest of the play. The wild determination obvious in Macbeth at the end of Scene 4 is remarked on by Hecat.

NOTES AND GLOSSARY

beldams:	hags
saucy:	impudent
close contriver:	secret inventor
wayward son:	(not a member of their circle)
Acheron:	hell
unto a dismal:	preparing for a disastrous
end:	purpose
profound:	heavy
sleights:	arts
spurn	ignore
security:	a sense of false security

Act III Scene 6

Lennox examines the recent 'accidents' and the evidence points to Macbeth's involvement. Macbeth has sent a rebuke to Macduff for his absence at the feast but Macduff has gone to England to rouse support against Macbeth. The opposition to Macbeth is growing.

COMMENTARY: Although this scene follows immediately on the previous one, we are given a sense of a stretch of time and, just as at the end of Act II, a larger perspective on events. The sense of Macbeth's tyranny, like a modern police state, is communicated very acutely in Lennox's analysis of events. He is ironic, oblique and somewhat guarded even if the implication of his remarks is quite clear. Macbeth is trying to tighten his hold on the country but the opposition is difficult to pin down and the English King, 'most pious Edward', is obviously prepared to help against Macbeth. Some intimation of Macduff's approaching tragedy is given in the final lines which connect with what Macbeth hinted at in the final lines of Scene 4.

NOTES AND GLOSSARY

hit:	agreed with
which ... further:	and you can draw your own conclusions
borne:	arranged
marry:	by Mary
want the thought:	fail to think
delinquents:	criminals
thralls:	slaves

'twere:	it were worth
broad:	frank
failed:	declined
due of birth:	the throne
malevolence ... **respect:**	his misfortunes lessen the high honour given to him
upon ... **aid:**	to help him
Northumberland:	on the Scottish border
ratify:	sanction
faithful:	honest
free:	(with no conditions attached)
cloudy:	frowning
rue:	regret
clogs:	burdens
to a caution:	to take care

Act IV Scene 1

The Witches prepare a foul concoction and arrange their spell. When Macbeth enters they agree to answer his enquiries and three Apparitions appear in order: an armed head, who warns Macbeth against Macduff; a bloody child who tells him that he cannot be harmed by one 'born of woman'; and a crowned child carrying a tree who guarantees Macbeth's safety until Birnam Wood comes to Dunsinane Hill. In answer to his question concerning Banquo's descendants, Macbeth is shown eight Kings ushered in by the spirit of Banquo. The Witches disappear and Lennox arrives with the news of Macduff's flight to England. Macbeth decides to kill every member of Macduff's family.

COMMENTARY: The Witches' broth is made as unpleasant and unchristian as possible to prepare the audience's minds for the arrival of Macbeth and to offer some parallel to the wickedness practised by Macbeth. Macbeth addresses the Witches almost familiarly and he 'conjures' them in their own manner. The Apparitions are obviously symbolic. The most straightforward interpretation sees the figures as (1) prophetic of the killed Macbeth, (2) the infant Macduff, and (3) young Malcolm coming to Dunsinane. Macbeth, typically, wishes to accept the favourable predictions and reject what is awkward for him and his horror at Banquo's ghost has much to do with his sense of powerlessness to prevent Banquo's family eventually succeeding to the throne. His impotent rage expresses itself in the pointless plan to massacre Macduff's family. As was noticeable in Act III, Scene 5, the

Witches are using Macbeth for their own purposes and Macbeth proves himself adaptable material even if in his better judgement he knows them to be evil and unreliable. The flight of Macduff seems to confirm their prophecies.

NOTES AND GLOSSARY

brinded:	streaky coloured
hedge-pig:	hedgehog
Harpier:	spirit of the witch
sweltered venom:	sweated poison
fenny:	slimy (from the marshes)
fork:	forked-tongue
howlet:	owl
mummy:	preserved body
maw and gulf:	belly and gullet
hemlock:	poisonous plant
yew:	(grown in churchyards)
eclipse:	(associated with catastrophes)
Jew, Turk, Tartar:	non-Christians
ditch-delivered:	born in a ditch
drab:	prostitute
slab:	slimy
chaudron:	entrails
pricking:	(omen of approaching evil)
yesty:	foaming
lodged:	beaten down
germens:	seeds
sicken:	be sick with its own work
farrow:	young pigs
gibbet:	the tree where the murderer is hanged
office:	your works
harped:	guessed
take a bond of fate:	guarantee the promise of fate by killing Macduff
round and top:	crown
chafes:	protests
Birnam ... Dunsinane:	places separated by ten miles
impress:	conscript
bodements:	prophecies
rebellious:	(against him and death) compare Act III, Scene 4, 70–2
lease of nature:	his natural lifetime
mortal custom:	natural death

eight kings:	the Stuart line leading to James I
sear:	burn
crack of doom:	the Last Day
glass:	mirror
two-fold ... sceptres:	symbols to show that they rule over England, Scotland and Ireland
boltered:	matted
antic:	fantastic
flighty:	fleeting
deed go with it:	we act immediately
firstlings:	first impulses
trace:	follow
sights:	apparitions

Act IV Scene 2

In Macduff's castle in Fife, Ross tries to explain to Lady Macduff why her husband has hurried off to England. She finds his desertion of his family impossible to justify. A stranger arrives as she is discussing the situation with her son, warns her to escape immediately, but he has barely departed when Macbeth's murderers break in and kill her and her son.

COMMENTARY: This scene has the moving quality of a particular family atrocity. Lady Macduff and her son are presented to us as pathetically vulnerable. The futility of Lady Macduff's condemnation of her husband's unexplained departure heightens our sense of her political innocence. Ross and the Messenger, fresh from the Court of Macbeth, know how tyranny operates and how the individual has to act secretly to survive. The glib cleverness of her young son has the same pathos. We know that Macbeth's agents are on their way and the discussion between mother and son is wasted breath.

NOTES AND GLOSSARY

make us traitors:	make us look like traitors
titles:	property
wants ... touch:	lacks ordinary affection
will fight:	will fight for
coz:	form of 'cousin'
school:	control
fits o' the season:	uncertainties of the time
hold rumour from:	believe rumours inspired by
things ... before:	(he says that the situation can only improve)

disgrace:	shame (because he would weep)
net ... gin:	traps to catch birds
wit:	cleverness
swears and lies:	swears an oath (promise) and then breaks it
enow:	enough
prattler:	chatterer
your state ... perfect:	I certainly know your noble rank
doubt:	suspect
homely:	humble
do worse:	(not to warn you)
fell:	savage
which:	(that is, the cruelty)
laudable:	praiseworthy
unsanctified:	unprotected
fry:	offspring

Act IV Scene 3

In the King of England's palace, Macduff describes the horrors of Macbeth's reign. Malcolm queries Macduff's political integrity and, when Macduff urges that Macbeth must be deposed he presents a picture of himself as worse even than Macbeth. Macduff shows his honesty by rejecting the idea of such a king and Malcolm admits that he has been testing Macduff's loyalty to Scotland and declares himself ready to lead an attack on Macbeth. The King of England is treating sick subjects and as Malcolm describes the cure to Macduff, Ross arrives with news of the slaughter of the Macduff family. After Macduff has expressed his grief it is agreed that the time has arrived for the attack on Macbeth.

COMMENTARY: This scene is longer and slower-moving than any other in the play. The main function of the scene is to assemble and assess the moral forces present in the drama before the final attack on Macbeth's corruption is launched. Malcolm, the murdered Duncan's son and claimant to the throne, and Macduff who remained with Macbeth but has led the internal opposition to him and we know that he has been punished for it—these two are appropriate characters to review the situation in Scotland and look forward to the possibility of a brighter future. The attack on evil must come when the forces of goodness are mobilised *and* the emotional intensity is right. The army is ready but the news of the brutal slaughter of Macduff's family signals the right moment.

NOTES AND GLOSSARY

mortal:	deadly
bestride ... birthdom:	defend our fallen native land
like ... dolour:	the same cry of sorrow
to friend:	propitious, convenient
sole:	very
deserve ... me:	gain from him by using me
and wisdom:	and it may be wise
recoil ... charge:	do something wicked if ordered to by the king
transpose:	alter
brightest:	Satan
rawness:	helpless condition
motives:	influences
jealousies:	suspicions
rightly just:	completely honest
check:	cross-examine
affeered:	confirmed
to boot:	in addition
fear:	doubt
withal:	moreover
England:	(the king)
grafted:	planted
confineless harms:	boundless evils
top:	surpass
luxurious:	lustful
sudden:	violent
voluptuousness:	lechery
continent:	restraining
convey:	indulge secretly
time ... hoodwink:	may deceive the people
to devour ... inclined:	(many will offer themselves to the king)
ill-composed affection:	wicked nature
staunchless:	limitless
forge:	invent
summer-seeming:	short-lived
foisons:	plenty
of ... own:	in your own possession
portable:	tolerable
division:	variations
several:	different
uproar:	destroy
untitled:	illegal

interdiction:	condemnation
blaspheme . . . breed:	slander his parents
died:	prepared for death
thy:	(the hope of his heart)
trains:	tricks
modest . . . me:	ordinary caution pulls me back
unspeak:	cancel
abjure:	reject
forsworn:	dishonest
at a point:	prepared
goodness:	success
be like . . . quarrel:	equal the justness of our cause
stay:	await
convinces:	is beyond
assay of art:	medical skill
presently:	immediately
Evil:	scrofula
here-remain:	stay
solicits:	persuades
strangely visited:	curiously afflicted
mere:	very
stamp:	coin
leaves:	hands down
benediction:	power, blessing
virtue:	power
speak:	proclaim
betimes:	quickly
marked:	noticed
modern ecstasy:	commonplace emotion
or . . . sicken:	before they have time to fall ill
nice:	elaborate
doth . . . speaker:	causes the teller to be booed
teems:	is born
niggard:	miser
witnessed:	evidenced
out:	in rebellion
doff:	remove
gives out:	can provide
latch:	catch
fee-grief:	individual sorrow
possess:	inform
surprised:	attacked suddenly

quarry: dead bodies
whispers . . . heart: whispers to the overburdened heart
hell-kite: bird of prey from hell
dam: mother
fell: savage
dispute: struggle against
naught: wicked
demerits: sins
whetstone: sharpener
play . . . eyes: weep
intermission: delay
too: (and me)
our . . . leave: we need only to take our leave
put . . . instruments: urge on their human agents

Act V Scene 1

In Dunsinane Castle a doctor and Lady Macbeth's lady-in-waiting are watching to see if Lady Macbeth walks in her sleep as her servant has reported to the doctor. She enters and begins to rub her hands as if struggling to clean them and before she departs she refers to the deaths of Duncan, Macduff's wife and Banquo. The doctor confesses that he is incapable of dealing with such cases.

COMMENTARY: We have not seen Lady Macbeth since Act III, Scene 4 and her behaviour in the present scene shows that her carefully contrived mask has slipped. In her sleep-walking she reveals the guilts and anxieties by which she is tortured. Particularly, she re-enacts the first murder scene when she took the initiative and organised a stumbling Macbeth. Now, alone, her loyalty to her husband remains intact; only once does she reproach him, 'No more o' that; you mar all with this starting'. Her behaviour is revealing and also very moving. She has given all and now her present is overwhelmed by the past. 'What's done cannot be undone'. A candle is no protection against murky Hell.

NOTES AND GLOSSARY
field: fighting
closet: chest
perturbation: upset
effects of watching: actions of one awake
meet: appropriate
lo: look

guise:	habit
close:	hidden
mar ... starting:	spoil everything with your nervousness
sorely charged:	heavily burdened
dignity:	worth
practice:	knowledge
abroad:	about
annoyance:	injury
mated:	bewildered

Act V Scene 2

Scottish rebel forces prepare to join with Malcolm's English army near Birnam Wood. Reports suggest that Macbeth is becoming more desperate and his support is deserting him.

COMMENTARY: A series of short scenes gives the impression of swift action and manoeuvring armies. Macbeth is being gradually isolated. Even his wife has been shown to have collapsed under the pressure and, as the besieging force strengthens, Macbeth is left more and more on his own. The description of him is parallel to the picture of his wife in the previous scene.

NOTES AND GLOSSARY

colours:	banners
power:	army
dear:	heartfelt
bleeding:	bloody
alarm:	call to battle
excite:	rouse
mortified:	dead
file:	list
unrough:	beardless
protest ... manhood:	want to show they are grown up
buckle ... cause:	keep control of his disorderly forces
minutely:	minute by minute
upbraid:	rebuke
faith-breach:	treachery
in:	because of
pestered senses:	tormented nerves
sickly weal:	diseased country
purge:	cleansing
dew:	nourish
sovereign flower:	(King Malcolm)

Act V Scene 3

Macbeth, besieged in Dunsinane Castle, puts a desperate trust in the Witches' predictions. He has become violent and inconsistent with his servants, despairing in himself. The doctor's diagnosis of Lady Macbeth's condition gives Macbeth no comfort but he asks the doctor to find a remedy for Scotland's situation.

COMMENTARY: Macbeth's conduct and speech have become wild. He repeats himself, contradicts himself and does not seem able to listen properly to what others say. When the doctor tells him about Lady Macbeth, Macbeth seems more concerned to shout at the doctor and demand a cure for his own situation than with a treatment for his wife. But behind the shouting, Macbeth realises that he is coming to the end of his resources, nobody is freely loyal to him and his shouting saves him from considering his situation calmly and realistically.

NOTES AND GLOSSARY

them:	the thanes
taint:	be infected
consequences:	developments
epicures:	luxury lovers
sway:	am moved
black:	at the time of the play the damned in hell were thought to be black
loon:	foolish boy
goose:	cowardly and stupid
prick ... fear:	make your face red by pinching it in order to hide your fear
lily-livered:	cowardly
patch:	fool
linen:	(white of cowardice)
counsellors:	encouragers
whey-face:	milk-white face
push:	crisis
chair:	establish
disseat:	unthrone
way:	course
sere:	withered condition
yellow:	(of autumn and dying)
mouth-honour:	lip-service
fain:	like to
skirr:	scour

thick-coming:	recurring
minister to:	treat
raze out:	erase
oblivious antidote:	cure that makes one forget
physic:	medical skill
staff:	spear
dispatch:	hurry
cast . . . land:	analyse the urine (of Scotland)
pristine:	fresh
pull't off:	(his armour)
rhubarb, cyme:	(purgative plants)
scour:	cleanse
it:	(some piece of his armour)
bane:	harm
profit:	money

Act V Scene 4

The army assembled against Macbeth is ordered by Malcolm to cut branches from Birnam Wood to disguise the number of soldiers. They march confidently towards Dunsinane.

COMMENTARY: The Witches' promise in which Macbeth put such trust is revealed as open to different meanings. The quiet confidence and the professionalism apparent in Malcolm's army are in sharp contrast to the shouting, boasting and disorganisation shown by Macbeth in the previous scene. All the Scottish nobles who have appeared earlier in the play are now allied against Macbeth.

NOTES AND GLOSSARY

chambers:	bedrooms
shadow:	conceal
discovery:	spies
err:	mistake (our numbers)
endure:	not prevent
our . . . before't:	us besieging it
advantage to be given:	opportunity to escape presents itself
more and less:	great and small
attend . . . event:	await the outcome
due decision:	certainty
owe:	actually possess
certain . . . arbitrate:	fighting must decide the actual result

Act V Scene 5

In the castle Macbeth is preparing to withstand the siege when he is told of his wife's death. As the emptiness of his life is brought home to him a messenger arrives with the news that Birnam Wood is approaching Dunsinane. He realises that all is lost but decides to die fighting.

COMMENTARY: It is possible that Macbeth's castle could withstand a long siege but there is a mixture of boasting, detachment from ordinary life and loss in his claim that he is now unmoved by fear. Lady Macbeth's death, possibly by her own hand, reduces his bravado and resolution to empty words. Life seems futile and deceptive (compare his false words in II.3.88–93). The report of Birnam Wood's movement confirms the deceptiveness of the Witches' advice to Macbeth. He can now submit quietly or fight on, knowing the futility of his struggle. He raises himself to fight. The future has no real meaning for him; as his life stands what lies ahead is a mere continuation of the present struggle.

NOTES AND GLOSSARY

them lie:	the besieging army stay
argue:	fever
farced:	reinforced
dareful:	boldy
cooled:	frozen (with fear)
night-shriek:	owl
fell of hair:	scalp
dismal treatise:	story of horror
direness:	horrors
start:	startle
she . . . hereafter:	she would have died sometime anyway, or she should have chosen some time in the future
time:	more appropriate time
petty pace:	slow speed
recorded time:	life (individual or human)
poor player:	unskilled actor
struts and frets:	performs boastfully and anxiously
signifying:	meaning, adding up to
watch:	guard
endure:	suffer
cling:	wither the flesh from your bones
pull in resolution:	check my confidence
fiend:	devil
avouches:	alleges

tarrying:	remaining
estate o' the world:	universe
wrack:	destruction
harness:	armour

Act V Scene 6

(Different editors divide the remainder of the play in different ways and it was considered more suitable in this book to deal with the remaining lines together)

Outside the castle the battle commences and Macbeth, surrounded, kills young Siward. He is sought out by Macduff while the defence of the castle collapses and finally Macbeth and Macduff prepare to fight. Macbeth claims that he is invulnerable but Macduff informs him that he was not 'born' to his mother in the usual way and in the fighting Macduff kills Macbeth. When Macduff brings Macbeth's head in front of the army Malcolm, accepted as the new king, pledges that he will bring peace and order back to Scotland.

COMMENTARY: Shakespeare tries to convey on the stage the action of the battle by having characters move on and off the centre of our attention. The focus of our attention is, of course, on Macbeth. He clings to the prophecy that he cannot be harmed by one born of a woman and fights accordingly with a curious nonchalance. Although his castle has fallen behind him he fights on and seems to accept the inevitability of defeat only when the circumstances of Macduff's birth show again that the Witches told only a partial truth. He fights to the death rather than accept humiliation and we are moved by the helplessness of his final struggle. The play ends with the restoration of the order Macbeth had disrupted and a reassertion of the Christian values that Macbeth had overthrown.

NOTES AND GLOSSARY

battle:	battalion
we:	(the royal we)
order:	plan
clamorous harbingers:	noisy announcers
stake:	pole (to which the bear was tied)
bear-like:	(baiting a tied bear with dogs was a popular sport)
course:	attack of the dogs
still:	for ever
kerns:	Irish mercenary soldiers
staves:	spears

undeeded:	unused
bruited:	announced
gently rendered:	surrendered without a struggle
strike beside us:	fight with us
play . . . fool:	commit suicide (honourable death for a defeated Roman general)
lives:	living men
charged:	burdened
terms . . . out:	words can describe you
losest:	waste
intrenchant:	unable to be cut
impress:	mark
crests:	helmets
charmed:	protected by magic
angel:	devil (bad angel)
untimely ripped:	abnormally delivered
cowed . . . man	made cowardly my manly spirit
juggling:	cheating
palter:	play(like equivocate)
gaze:	display
painted:	advertised
baited:	tormented (like the bear)
rabble:	crowd
opposed:	against me
try the last:	fight to the death
would:	wish
go off:	die
prowess confirmed:	his bravery confirmed (that he was a man)
unshrinking station:	place from which he did not retreat
before:	on his front
knell is knolled:	death is announced
parted . . . score:	died nobly and contributed his share
time:	people
compassed . . . pearl:	surrounded by your nobles
expense:	extent
reckon . . . loves:	reward your individual services
snares:	traps
producing forth:	bringing to trial
ministers:	agents
needful . . . us:	other necessary things demand our attention
by the grace of Grace:	with the help of God
in measure:	correctly

Part 3

Commentary

Occasion and sources

In 1603 James VI of Scotland became James I, King of Scotland, England and Ireland. He was a vain man, undignified, scholarly after a fashion, a generous patron of the arts. 'Kings', he said, 'are not only God's lieutenants upon earth and sit upon God's throne, but even by God himself they are called gods'. Certain it is that James believed himself to have special virtues and powers because he was king. From 1604 onwards he touched people against the Evil (a skin disease called scrofula) and attributed his success to prayer. The passage in *Macbeth*, Act IV, Scene 3, lines 140–159 appears to be a direct description of this practice. His interest in witchcraft and heresy is also catered for in the play. His life had been threatened by a group of witches in Scotland in 1591 and in 1605 the Gunpowder Plot had sought to blow up his government. Undoubtedly part of the concern in *Macbeth* with witchcraft and equivocation (see the Porter's speech in Act II, Scene 3) relates to the topicality of these issues which the audience, and particularly King James, knew about from the trials resulting from the two plots. In 1601, Essex, and in 1603, Raleigh, two most distinguished nobles, were tried for treason and sentenced to execution.

Shakespeare in the 1590s wrote nine plays dealing with England's dynastic history. These history plays cover a large span of time and examine a wide diversity of incident and experience. Although it is a serious over-simplification to see these plays as crude propaganda for the legitimacy of Elizabeth's position as Queen, yet it is an undeniable truth that they were written at a very special time and appealed to patriotic, Protestant Englishmen in a very special way. The wicked Richard III who seized the throne and held it by cruelty and deception was a cautionary example of the danger of a bad king. The young, irresponsible Henry became, on the death of his father, Henry V and found qualities in himself which made him a popular and heroic king. Many of Shakespeare's plays examine situations of political ambitions and power. The setting may be Rome, Alexandria, Ancient Britain, Denmark, fifteenth century England, or eleventh century Scotland, and never before had a dramatist journeyed so widely for his material, but the repeated investigation indicates the contemporary fascination with the subject of political order and disorder.

For *Macbeth*, Shakespeare used the same source-book as he had used for the English history plays, Holinshed's *Chronicles of England, Scotland and Ireland* which was reprinted in 1587. Shakespeare never followed Holinshed slavishly but created plays based on material he found in the *Chronicles*. In the case of *Macbeth* some of the main differences from Holinshed cast some light on Shakespeare's intentions in writing the play. The action of the play is more tightly organised than the collection of incidents that his source offers; the characters are differentiated and developed in a manner completely unlike the original; Duncan is made into a good king and Macbeth into an almost totally brutal king; Banquo, the ancestor of King James, becomes an honest man whereas in Holinshed he helps Macbeth to murder Duncan; greater prominence is given to the Witches; the sense of time and location is altered to suggest a concentration of action.

Structure of the play

By the 'structure' of a play we mean how the whole play is made up of its parts and how these parts relate to each other. A play is not a gallery of portraits (the characters) not is it a series of incidents (the plot) although both of these elements are very important. Even in a play as rich in incident as *Macbeth*, we learn most about the meaning, the total impact, of a play through the dialogue.

Macbeth is the third shortest play written by Shakespeare and one of the immediately striking aspects of it is the speed at which the action occurs. It was mentioned above that Shakespeare reorganises the stories concerning Macbeth and the other characters as he found them related in Holinshed. A number of battles involving various people over a considerable period of time are concentrated in Act I of the play into the sustained heroism of Macbeth. Always, throughout the play, the focus of our attention is fixed firmly on Macbeth. For example, in Act I, Scene 5 Macbeth does not appear till after line 50 but it is his letter that Lady Macbeth reads to us and it is his character that she analyses. In Act IV, Scene 3, set in the English Court, where we have a long discussion between Macduff and Malcolm on the subjects of loyalty and good kings, Macbeth is never out of our minds. We know what he has done to Macduff's family, we can see that the invented portrait Malcolm offers of himself is really a description of Macbeth, we hear the contrast between the 'good king' (Edward) and the evil Macbeth. However distant from each they may be in actual geographical terms, in the play Fife, Forres, Inverness, Scone, Dunsinane, Glamis are all brought within one day's riding time of each other and yet, because of the sense we are given of the state of Scotland and the Kingship of Scotland, the size of Macbeth's ambition and the participation of the whole natural world, we feel that the struggle in the play involves a whole country and beyond that the soul of mankind. No sooner do the Witches voice a prophecy than it is fulfilled; no sooner does Macbeth inform his wife of the Witches' prophecy and she considers the possibilities than the Messenger arrives with the news that the King comes to spend the night. In the final act the stretch of time from Lady Macbeth's sleep-walking to Macbeth's death seems to last only as long as it takes us to read the pages. This compression of time heightens our excitement and sense of suspense.

Unlike many of Shakespeare's plays, *Macbeth* has no sub-plot, or secondary action. The concentration of the play is on Macbeth. How is it, then, that the play offers so much more than the analysis of one man? One reason for this lies in the way Shakespeare juxtaposes what, in cinema terms, would be called close-up shots and longer-range shots. Shakespeare uses the lesser characters to comment on the central action, to give a wider context to Macbeth's behaviour. Each act, with the exception of Act I, ends with such a scene where we are helped to take stock of the situation. Act III, Scene 6, will serve as an example. Lennox and the unnamed Lord are not in themselves important to the play but they act as a pressure gauge to measure the tyranny of Macbeth and to register the wider significance of Macbeth's evil. The scenes with Duncan and later with Malcolm are presented as examples of decent kingly order against which Macbeth is to be judged. Equally, the scenes with the Witches show an abyss of anti-human evil on the edge of which mankind stumbles and into which Macbeth enters.

The play operates as a series of contrasts and parallels. One of the subtlest elements in the texture of the play and one which it is crucial that we notice is the use of dramatic irony. Dramatic irony occurs when a line uttered by a character has a secondary meaning noticed by the audience but not by the speaker or when a statement or action has a special significance to the audience because of what the audience knows has happened already or anticipates will happen. Some examples should help to explain how this operates. In Act I, Scene 4, lines 12–15 King Duncan says

> There's no art
> To find the mind's construction in the face.
> He was a gentleman on whom I built
> An absolute trust.

Enter Macbeth, Banquo, Ross and Angus
> O worthiest cousin!

Duncan is talking about the treacherous Cawdor; but we know from the previous scene what thoughts are in Macbeth's mind and we apply Duncan's words to Macbeth as he enters. Duncan does not realise the full truth of his own words: the 'worthiest cousin' has prepared a most trustworthy face. In Act II, Scene 2, line 67, Lady Macbeth affirms 'A little water clears us of this deed.' Later, in Act V, Scene 1, walking in her sleep and making the movements of washing her hands, the conscience-tormented Lady Macbeth asks 'What, will these hands ne'er be clean?' (line 42). When we come on the later line we remember the earlier statement and we appreciate the collapse that has taken place. If we know the play already, when we come to the line in Act II our minds move ahead to Act V and we anticipate her collapse and realise how flimsy is her self-control during the murder of Duncan.

Immediately after the murder of Duncan comes the Porter scene (Act II, Scene 3). There are obscurities in this scene, possibly because of topical references readily understandable to Shakespeare's own audience, but the main points of the scene are clear enough. The Porter imagines himself as the gate-keeper of Hell and we see the ironic truth of such a claim because Macbeth has indeed made his castle a hell. The central word of the Porter's rambling talk is 'equivocator'. He welcomes to Hell various deceivers, people who have played with the truth to suit their own purposes, and we recognise Macbeth as the absolute equivocator of the play, particularly in this very scene where his elaborate words seem horribly deceitful. The irony of these cross-references, however, does not stop there. In Act V when the prophecies of the Witches which promised such safety have been exposed, Macbeth concedes that he has been the victim of equivocation as well as its instrument. In Scene 5, lines 42–4 his confidence slips:

> *I pull in resolution, and begin*
> *To doubt the equivocation of the fiend*
> *That lies like truth*

Later in Scene 6, line 58, the Witches have become 'these juggling fiends'. The Porter acts as an oblique commentator on the murder and Macbeth's descent into Hell. The very roughness and comedy of his act increases the gruesomeness of the murder.

Imagery

In a good play the dramatist seeks to make the ideas, characters and developments vivid and memorable. One way of achieving this aim is to associate, for example, a character with certain things, qualities or activities so that, when these occur, the audience remembers the character and comes to a fuller understanding of him. In Shakespeare's later plays, particularly, the imagery (that is, the groups of associative images) is a very important element, giving the texture of the plays density and richness. Some images, of course, are striking individually but it is more rewarding to see the imagery as functioning in strands which help to connect, reinforce and enliven the shifts in the play as a whole. The richness of Shakespeare's imagery must inevitably suffer in translation and some is certainly lost to modern English.

The idea of contrasts lies at the heart of *Macbeth* and we intend to concentrate only on some of the strands of imagery that substantiate this interpretation. Other strands which can be followed fruitfully are those concerned with the themes of deceit, unnaturalness, killings, innocence and obligation.

Order and Health opposed by Disorder and Sickness

In Act I, Scene 4 we have a scene of royal order when King Duncan, pleased with his success in the battle, distributes justice and rewards. Great emphasis is placed on the ties that bind a subject to his king and mutual trust is ceremoniously communicated. At the end of the scene, Duncan says (of Macbeth):

> *And in his commendations I am fed;*
> *It is a banquet to me. Let's after him*
> *Whose care is gone before to bid us welcome.*
> *It is a peerless kinsman*
>
> (lines 56–9)

Gradually through the play we come to recognise 'banquets' as an image of order. After the supper in Macbeth's castle Duncan is described by Banquo as having been 'in unusual pleasure' (line 13) and he is now 'in measureless content'. In Act III, Scene 1 Macbeth issues a special invitation to Banquo to 'a solemn supper' and when the supper begins in Scene 4 the new king is careful about the formal arrangements and the guests sit according to their 'degrees'. An intimation of disorder comes in the form of the Murderer with blood on his face, hardly a suitable guest, and when Macbeth rebukes the absent Banquo he brings disorder to the table. The supper is broken up by Lady Macbeth's command:

> *Stand not upon the order of your going;*
> *But go at once*
>
> (lines 118–119)

The unnamed Lord in Scene 6 of Act III prays that

> *we may again*
> *Give to our tables meat, sleep to our nights,*
> *Free from our feasts and banquets bloody knives.*
> *Do faithful homage and receive free honours*
> (lines 33–6)

In Act IV, Scene 3 Malcolm enumerates the kingly virtues (lines 92–4) and King Edward is obviously presented as an example of a good king whose personal qualities are matched by his ability to make his people healthy. It is from this court of good order that Malcolm sets out to bring back 'wholesome days' to Scotland and the discipline and dedication evident in his army are in contrast to the morale in Dunsinane Castle.

Throughout the play there occur images of disorder and sickness. From the 'hurly-burly' of the first scene, through the 'revolt' and 'broil' of the battle to the sense of hallucination with the Witches we are presented with disturbances of a calm. Drunkenness is important in the first two Acts (see Act I, Scene 7, line 35; Act II, Scene 1, line 31; Act II, Scene 2, lines 1–2; and the Porter scene) and we hear of Macbeth having a 'heat oppressed brain' and being 'brain-sickly' in the same acts. In Act III, Scene 1, line 106 Macbeth tells the Murderers that [we] 'wear our health but sickly in his [Banquo's] life' and in the following scene his wife tries to comfort him, saying 'things without all remedy/Should be without regard.' His mind is 'full of scorpions' and he is determined to bring ruin on the universe,

> *Ere we will eat our meal in fear, and sleep*
> *In the affliction of these terrible dreams*
> *That shake us nightly.*
> (III. 2. 17–19)

Two scenes later his lack of inner control becomes public in his 'solemn supper' when his vision of Banquo's ghost reduces him to a nervous wreck so that he breaks the 'good meeting'. Such symptoms continue throughout the remainder of the play and are shared by Lady Macbeth whose repressed conscience gives way in her sleep-walking scene.

Macbeth's personal condition is reflected in the disorder in nature on the night of Duncan's murder (see Act II, Scene 4, and subsequently in a sickness in the kingdom of Scotland described to Lady Macduff by Ross (Act IV, Scene 2, lines 15–22) and to Malcolm by Macduff (Act IV, Scene 3, lines 4–8). The Doctor, of whom Macbeth makes such impossible demands later, says in Act V, Scene 1, lines 67–8, 'unnatural deeds/Do breed unnatural troubles' and his diagnosis describes accurately the situation where the personal disorder of the king who 'cannot buckle his distempered cause/Within the belt of rule' is reflected in his country and in the world of nature.

Light and Grace opposed by Darkness and Evil

(Grace is used in its Christian sense of the helping power of God)
From the moral confusion suggested by the Witches' 'Fair is foul, and foul is fair' at the beginning, the play gradually moves to show the irreconcilable distinction between good and evil. When in Act I, Scene 4, lines 42–3, Duncan pronounces that 'signs of nobleness, like stars, shall shine/On all deservers', he is immediately challenged by Macbeth's private prayer:

> *Stars, hide your fires,*
> *Let not light see my black and deep desires.*
> *The eye wink at the hand; yet let that be*
> *Which the eye fears, when it is done, to see.*
>
> (lines 51–4)

In Act I, Scene 5, line 59 Lady Macbeth promises to Macbeth that there shall be no sun for Duncan in the morning as a result of 'this night's great business.' Just before Macbeth enters, his wife, in words reminiscent of his in the previous scene, prays,

> *Come, thick night,*
> *And pall thee in the dunnest smoke of hell,*
> *That my keen knife see not the wound it makes,*
> *Nor heaven peep through the blanket of the dark*
> *To cry, 'Hold, hold!'*
>
> (I. 5. 48–52)

Macbeth is well aware of the sinfulness of his plan to murder Duncan and in his soliloquy in Scene 7 he recognises the purity of Duncan who is 'so clear in his great office' that 'his virtues/Will plead like angels' against Macbeth's use of the 'poisoned chalice', an act of complete sacrilege. (See glossary on 'chalice')

It is easier to trace the two sets of imagery separately but it is of fundamental importance to appreciate that they comment on each other, they together emphasise the moral force of the play in the manner shown in the previous paragraph. In Macbeth's description of the murder, the sons of the king pray for God's blessing and in Macduff's description of the murdered Duncan he is 'the Lord's anointed temple'. Banquo, who at the beginning of Act II asked for the help of the

'merciful powers' against wicked thoughts now after the murder states
'In the great hand of God I stand' (Act II, Scene 3, line 127).

In Act III, Scene 6, line 27 we are told that Malcolm has been
welcomed by 'the most pious Edward with such a grace' and the Scottish
noblemen pray that a 'holy angel' will help to bring a blessing on
Scotland. Again as in the case of the order-disorder imagery, Act IV,
Scene 3 is very important in emphasising the difference between foulness
and grace; in particular, Malcolm's words, lines 19–24, the description
of King Edward, noted for his sanctity, and Macduff's confession of his
sinfulness in lines 220–6, all demonstrate that the forces against Macbeth trust in different powers (line 237) from his dark guides.

The contrary images of darkness and evil are particularly obvious in
the Witches, shrewdly observed by Banquo in Act I, Scene 3 to be 'the
instruments of darkness'. How quickly we find Macbeth invoking the
foulest spirits and darkening out his conscience with images of sorcery
and evil. His words immediately before the murder indicate clearly why
he cannot say 'amen' during the murder. Banquo's suspicion that
Macbeth has 'played most foully' to become king revives echoes of the
earlier instances of 'foul' and if he were to have overheard Macbeth's
self-commitment to darkness (Act III, Scene 2, lines 40–56) he would
have understood just how foul Macbeth's mind has become. By Act III,
Scene 4, after the disruption of the supper, Macbeth is stuck between
darkness and day (lines 125–6) or, as he puts it,

> *I am in blood*
> *Stepped in so far, that, should I wade no more,*
> *Returning were as tedious as go o'er*
> (lines 135–7)

Macbeth's self-identification with evil seems complete when in Act IV,
Scene 3 he conjures the Witches to answer his enquiries; the 'secret,
black, and midnight hags' are the instruments of evil and unnaturalness
as their brew has told us and they are addressed familiarly by something
they recognise as wicked (line 45). In Act V, Scene 1 Lady Macbeth
concedes in her dreams that 'Hell is murky'; she who had invoked 'thick
night' now requires 'light by her continually'. The Doctor declares the
case needs a divine care but Macbeth, obviously in a similar condition,
is beyond repentance, and claims that he is beyond fear.

In the final scene of the play we find Macbeth described as a 'devil'
(line 18), 'hellhound' (line 42), a follower of Satan (line 53) and a
'rarer monster'. Macbeth has killed Young Siward, a soldier of God,
according to his father who sees the war against Macbeth as a holy war
against evil.

The two strands of imagery of order and grace are completed in the final lines of the play which mark the defeat of disorder and evil:

> *and what needful else*
> *That calls upon us, by the grace of Grace*
> *We will perform in measure, time and place.*
> *So thanks to all at once, and to each one,*
> *Whom we invite to see us crowned at Scone.*

Verse and style

Macbeth is, for the most part, written in blank verse. The basic unit of blank verse is a line in iambic pentameter without a rhyme scheme but, increasingly in his plays, Shakespeare's use of the line and the number of its syllables and stresses became freer. A strict iambic pentameter has ten syllables with the stress falling on the even ones, for example, 'And wakes it now to look so green and pale'. Shakespeare's verse is seldom as regular as this but the pattern is there below the changing surface giving regularity with flexibility. The sense and the punctuation do not stop dead at the end of lines but often cross into the following line, giving a feeling of the unevenness of spoken English. By grouping stressed syllables Shakespeare catches the emphasis and intensity of a character, for example,

> *Whiles níghts bláck ágents to their préys do róuse*

where Macbeth's grim fascination with nastiness is brought out by the voice stress on 'night's black agents'. Occasionally, Shakespeare uses rhyming couplets. A considerable number of scenes intimate their conclusion by this means but there are two other significant uses of rhyme. The Witches commonly speak in rhyme, often using a shorter line and a different stress pattern to give a sound of incantations and charms. More interesting is the fact that Macbeth uses rhyming couplets more often than any other character and more than the heroes of Shakespeare's other tragedies. It does seem that he has an affinity with the Witches.

Prose in Shakespeare's plays often denotes the low social rank of a character, or it occurs in a situation which is abnormal, in some way, to the ordinary behaviour of the play. In *Macbeth* there are four situations where prose is used: Macbeth's letter to his wife, Act I, Scene 5; the Porter scene, Act II, Scene 3; the conversation between Lady Macduff and her son, Act IV, Scene 2; and the sleep-walking scene, Act V, Scene 1. The letter being in prose requires no explanation. What have the other three scenes in common? They all present characters who seem artless or in a state of mind where verse would appear contrived. The Porter can ramble on in his rude, somewhat incoherent way because of the amount of alcohol still in him; the mother and her child, talking of birds and traitors and fathers soften from the formality of verse to the affectionate slackness of prose but revert to verse when strangers enter; in her sleep-walking, Lady Macbeth loses the customary controls of verse and talks 'straight' for the first time in the play and her attendants, lower in the social scale, can talk in verse only when she has departed.

Shakespeare's characters do not voice his opinions, they speak out of their dramatic situation. That is, to understand fully a speech or an exchange of dialogue it is necessary to hear the words in their context in the play. It is impossible to deduce what Shakespeare's attitude to life was from reading Macbeth's speech in Act V, Scene 5 beginning 'Tomorrow, and tomorrow, and tomorrow'. Two examples from lesser characters in different parts of the play are offered to demonstrate how necessary it is to read these pieces with proper attention to their style and context.

The first is from Act I, Scene 2 where Duncan is receiving reports from the battle fronts. The Captain is introduced to us as a 'bloody man' straight from the fight and he spends over forty lines describing the struggle of Macbeth against heavy odds. His style of reporting is breathless, lavish but crudely put together. He is weak from loss of blood and fatigue and his syntax is inelegant and transitions from one point to the next are sudden. But his manner is arresting—'Mark, King of Scotland, mark!'—and at least three dramatic functions are served well by his speech. One, the play moves off (from the short scene with the Witches) to a very exciting start; two, he comes across as the epitome of the honest, somewhat brutal soldier; three, and most important in the long term, he introduces us to Macbeth, a hero of battle, brave but a slaughterer. Contrast the manner of speech of Ross seven lines later, smoothly put together, restrained, telling what he had done for the cause of the King.

The second example is the speech of Lennox in Act III, Scene 6, lines 1–20. The studied quality of the syntax tells much about the mentality of the speaker and much about the general climate of secrecy and spying in Macbeth's country. Notice the rhetorical questions to which he provides a knowing answer. We can hear the dry ironic tone of voice of the character as he speaks. Nothing is stated directly but the speech is full of words of apparent opinion: 'gracious', 'valiant', 'monstrous', 'damned', 'pious', 'nobly', 'wisely', and so on. Macbeth's methods of deceit and sly viciousness have entered into the manner of speech of those around him. It is significant that Lennox is still serving Macbeth in Act IV, Scene 1, where he says 'What's your grace's will?' and 'No, my lord' and 'Ay, my good lord'.

Characters

'Character' in a play, particularly in a Shakespearean play, is a difficult term to delimit. In a sense all the people, the parts, in a play are characters and that is what is meant by 'list of characters' or 'dramatis personae'. Not all parts, however, are equal; some are longer than others but, it may be, less important to the essential action and core of the play. Julius Caesar, for example, is not a large part in the play of that name but he influences the action throughout the play. Banquo has only a third of the lines of Malcolm but we could argue that he is a more important character because we are more aware of him, his being impinges on the action throughout the play. By character here we mean a person's essential qualities as these are manifest in the dialogue and action and as they operate in helping to create the total effect of the play.

Shakespeare's plays are not like modern novels where the author spends a great deal of time helping us to understand how a character has come to be what he is. Often we have to accept what we are given in a Shakespearean play without asking too many questions about how the situation has been reached. The use, however, of asides and soliloquies in which a character voices his private thoughts to the audience but not to the other characters is one important way in which character is revealed. There is a psychological depth and truth in a Shakespearean play but there are also many aspects which remain untouched.

Macbeth

In the reports of Macbeth's courage in battle in the second scene of the play, he is 'brave Macbeth', 'valour's minion', and Duncan, acknowledging his champion, calls him 'valiant cousin', 'noble Macbeth'. In Act I there is only one reservation expressed about Macbeth's character and in different circumstances it could be considered a compliment. This 'peerless kinsman' to King Duncan is judged by his wife to have a nature 'too full o' the milk of human-kindness' (Scene 5, line 15) to allow him to kill Duncan. She recognises his ambition to be 'great' but feels that he would prefer to be given the throne by someone else whatever methods were used, rather than grab it himself. The second part of her analysis points to a basic dishonesty in Macbeth and it is this aspect of his character that she ruthlessly attacks to overcome his doubts in Scene 7. His qualms and repulsion before and after Duncan's murder are denounced as cowardice and foolishness by his wife and later, in Act III, she feels he has not improved.

Macduff at the end of Act II appears to anticipate Banquo's suspicions that Macbeth has 'playedst most foully' to gain the throne. By the end of Act III the decline in Macbeth's reputation is obvious; his title of the second half of the play, 'tyrant', has been introduced. From now on there is not a good word uttered about Macbeth. Macduff claims that,

> *Not in the legions*
> *Of horrid hell can come a devil more damned*
> *In evils to top Macbeth*

and Malcolm asserts

> *I grant him bloody,*
> *Luxurious, avaricious, false, deceitful,*
> *Sudden, malicious, smacking of every sin*
> *That has a name*

At the end the 'cursed head' of the 'dead butcher' is displayed.

Macbeth is a soldier in armour at his first appearance in the play and at his final exit. In between, we witness some very unsoldierly behaviour when he is frequently out of rational control, 'rapt' and 'brain sickly' earlier on, 'sick at heart' and 'cowed' towards the end. In situation after situation he is preoccupied with speculations and his awareness of this tendency leads to such resolutions as:

> *Strange things I have in head, that will to hand;*
> *Which must be acted ere they may be scanned*
>
> (III.4.138–9)

This comes at the end of the supper scene where he has undergone excruciating tortures in his mind at the appearance of Banquo's ghost. He can act only when he does not allow himself to think and, as a result, his actions become more frenzied as the play continues. Only in Duncan's murder does he participate directly and then only under the inflexible pressure of his wife. After Duncan's and Banquo's murders come the scenes where his horror and conscience force themselves into his conscious mind to the neglect of all else. In the case of the murder of Macduff's family we do not see Macbeth again for over four hundred lines after he says, 'To crown my thoughts with acts, be it thought and done' and the terrifying callousness of the crime seems beyond his own comprehension. Each murder he commits or commissions is expected by him to end the 'restless ecstacy' he suffers but even before Duncan's murder he sees something of the futility of such an effort when he realises,

> *that we but teach*
> *Bloody instructions, which, being taught, return*
> *To plague the inventor.*
> (I.7.8–10)

Caught in a labyrinth of his own making there is a pathetic desperation in his blustering commands:

> *There is not flying hence nor tarrying here.*
> *I' gin to be aweary of the sun,*
> *And wish the estate o' the world were now undone—*
> *Ring the alarum bell!—Blow wind, come wrack,*
> *At least we'll die with harness on our back.*
> (V.5.48–52)

Macbeth lays bare his thoughts in asides through the play and his confusion is apparent from very early on:

> *This supernatural soliciting*
> *Cannot be ill, cannot be good*
> (I.3.129–130)

and

> *Function is smothered in surmise*
> *And nothing is but what is not*
> (lines 140–1)

We are presented with a man motivated to kill Duncan only because of ambition but who, having yielded to this desire, steps so far into blood that there is no turning back. As the play progresses we are made aware of his peculiar isolation as all escape routes are blocked off. Before Banquo's murder he tells only a certain amount of his plans to his wife who had been his 'dearest partner of greatness' and without her his reliance on the Witches becomes greater. He recognises in Act V, Scene 3 that:

> *that which should accompany old age,*
> *As honour, love, obedience, troops of friends,*
> *I must not look to have*
> (lines 24–6)

For him, 'supped full with horrors', his wife dead, his support deserting him, life has lost all rational meaning:

> *It is a tale*
> *Told by an idiot, full of sound and fury,*
> *Signifying nothing.*
>
> (V.5.26–8)

We have noted earlier (page 61) Macbeth's association with darkness and evil, we have heard the opinions of those around him, we have witnessed his actions, and in all he is a villain. How is it, then, that we retain an interest in, possibly even a sympathy for, Macbeth? The answer must lie in the weight of evidence about him presented from the inside. We hear from his own heart of his ambition, his weakness, the wrongness of his behaviour, his deceits, and we are made aware of the intoxication he feels at his own evil. Macbeth, as a man, is weak and he finds a spurious strength in his viciousness. In his dialogue we notice a shift from a diplomatic, hollow ornateness to a blustering, bullying language full of exclamations, questions, commands but equally hollow. In the final act Macbeth concedes to himself that his strutting and fretting are empty gestures but, chained as he is like a bear, he will not surrender and we cannot but admire his affirmation that he 'will try the last'.

Lady Macbeth

No background is offered to explain Macbeth's ambition to be king and there is a similar abruptness in the nature of Lady Macbeth as she appears in Act I, Scene 5. When she reads of the Witches' prophecy in Macbeth's letter there is no indication of doubt, suspicion, hesitation in her reaction. Her one worry concerns Macbeth's ability to fulfil or enact the prophecy and she is confident that the 'valour of my tongue' will persuade him. By the time Macbeth arrives several minutes later she has mobilised her whole being towards the task of Duncan's murder. She is prepared to sacrifice her femininity and her humanity to 'give solely sovereign sway and masterdom' to Macbeth and herself.

In all the public scenes in the play she acts 'like the innocent flower'; in the private scenes we see the 'serpent under't'. Her absoluteness of purpose, her discipline, her control of the situation are immaculate and we, like Macbeth, are morally paralysed by her power of will. In Act I, Scene 7 we see Macbeth's feeble questions and attempts to draw back smashed aside by counter questions and a mixture of violence and practicality which forces Macbeth into sharing her resolution and chiming in with her attitudes and words. In the scene of the murder there is a sharp contrast between the rambling, whining narration of Macbeth and the snapping, categorical rebukes and practical detail of his wife. Macbeth is stuck in his own imagination; she refuses to see anything but the immediate actions.

She manages to maintain this control over herself during the supper scene with Banquo's ghost but earlier in Act III, Scene 2 we have heard her first private thought since the murder of Duncan:

> *Naught's had, all's spent,*
> *Where our desire is got without content.*
> *'Tis safer to be that which we destroy*
> *Than by destruction dwell in doubtful joy.*

Macbeth enters at this point and she changes her attitude immediately, attempting to eradicate in Macbeth what we know she feels in herself. It is noticeable in this scene that after her initial words of comfort, she is allowed no time to speak by Macbeth and for the first time we hear her say 'What's to be done?' She does not know of Macbeth's plans for Banquo and planning has passed from her hands to Macbeth.

After the supper scene—where, incidentally, we notice after the departure of the guests Macbeth again shows his leadership—Lady Macbeth appears only once, in her sleep-walking scene at the beginning of Act V. This scene is very important to the play structurally because it summarises the murders of Macbeth before Malcolm's assault and the confession comes from his 'fiend-like queen' herself. But the question that intrigues readers is: Why has Lady Macbeth collapsed from her position in Act I? What has happened to the rigid self-discipline? The answer seems to lie in the very rigidity of her self-discipline. Macbeth, who started from a weaker position, has had some release in his own imaginings; he has confessed to the ugliness of his deeds and has gradually come to accept his precarious stance. His wife has only once in our hearing suggested that her contentment is incomplete. Gradually, in her case, her repressed conscience and her knowledge that the 'sovereign sway and masterdom' have not materialised have forced themselves into her dreams so that now, as the doctor says, she re-enacts the murders in her mind in sleep. The contrast between her curt assurance in Act II, Scene 2 and her foulness in Act V, Scene 1, is painfully ironic. Her suicide is the final desperate act of the mind seeking to cleanse itself:

> *Tis safer to be that which we destroy*
> *Than by destruction dwell in doubtful joy.*

Banquo

For the first half of the play, Banquo is very obviously presented by Shakespeare as a parallel figure to Macbeth. Both distinguish themselves in fighting for their king, both have promises made to them by the Witches, but there the similarity ends. Banquo's reply to the King's praise is brief and self-effacing; Macbeth's is fuller and, from our knowledge of Macbeth's thoughts in the previous scene, we suspect it is dishonest.

In the previous scene, Act I, Scene 3, Banquo's reaction to the Witches is noticeably more casual than Macbeth's but he does ask the Witches if they see anything in the future for him. In their equivocal replies they promise him greatness and happiness of some sort in comparison with Macbeth. In the play he is morally greater than Macbeth and he is not unhappy in the tortured manner of Macbeth. Their significant prediction, however, is that his descendants will become kings. Both men are genuinely startled at the immediate fulfilment of the Witches' prediction that Macbeth will become Thane of Cawdor but Banquo's puzzlement takes the form of scepticism and a deep distrust of the Witches whom he sees as the 'devil' or the 'instruments of darkness'. This distrust later becomes fear when, in Act II, Scene 1, he tells of the 'cursed thoughts that nature gives way to in repose' and we find out in line 20 that he has been dreaming of the Witches. Unlike Macbeth, he prays for God's help ('merciful powers') against whatever 'cursed thoughts' he has. In Christian doctrine sin takes place when temptation is yielded to, not when temptation occurs. We have seen Macbeth examining his temptation in his soliloquy at the beginning of the previous scene, but by the time Banquo is in bed, it is obvious to the audience that Macbeth is entering knowingly into a world of darkness and sorcery.

Macbeth is taunted by two aspects of Banquo which he explains in Act III, Scene 1, lines 48–71. The virtue, the strength of character of Banquo is a rebuke to Macbeth's weaker character and Macbeth cannot tolerate the thought that he has sacrificed his soul to profit Banquo by allowing his descendants to become kings. These two aspects remain to torment Macbeth's mind after the murder of Banquo and the escape of Fleance. Banquo's ghost arrives when summoned by Macbeth's conscience: when Macbeth tries to dismiss Banquo with words, the ghost comes to rebuke him. Macbeth's impotent rage at the survival of Banquo's line in the Witches' Show of eight kings expresses itself in the massacre of Macduff's 'wife, his babes, and all unfortunate souls/That trace him in his line'.

The Witches

The Witches are the instruments of malevolent forces which seek to lead men away from goodness. Macbeth is peculiarly vulnerable to their influence because he hears them voice the desires of his mind and after his initial fear at being caught out (Act I, Scene 3, lines 50–51) his mind moves easily along the route they indicate towards the 'imperial theme'. The Witches' nature is continually evoked and invoked in speeches by Macbeth and Lady Macbeth and their very sexlessness (Act I, Scene 3, lines 44–6) seems to correspond with Lady Macbeth's prayer against her own nature in Act I, Scene 5, lines 38–52.

Macbeth is able to find them when he chooses later on but he wants to hear only what favours himself. Too late he comes to realise that the Witches have their own purposes into which men fit and which men can serve. The equivocation theme which is central to the play operates most obviously through the Witches and they are the most striking voices of unnaturalness and disorder. Lady Macbeth offers no comment on the Witches, the 'metaphysical aid' who promise so much to her husband. It is Macbeth who needs the Witches to tell him what is in his own mind but is afraid to acknowledge it as his own. The Witches, of course, do not make promises; they utter riddles which Macbeth in his weakness interprets in his own apparent interest. He is, therefore, deceived not by the Witches but by his illfounded reliance on his own interpretation.

> *He shall spurn fate, scorn death, and bear*
> *His hopes, 'bove wisdom, grace and fear*
> *And you all know security*
> *Is mortal's chiefest enemy*
> (III.5.30–3)

Macduff

With his knocking at the gate, Macduff is the first intrusion of the outside world on Macbeth's murder of Duncan. Through the remainder of the play he continues to annoy and challenge Macbeth and in Act II, Scene 4, lines 37–8 we hear the first suspicion of Macbeth when Macduff, having decided not to attend Macbeth's coronation, suggests that the new regime may not be a comfortable one. He keeps clear of Macbeth's 'solemn supper' and at the end of the supper scene Macbeth's plans of further murders seem to include the uncooperative Macduff, plans which receive confirmation from his visit to the Witches. Shake speare's handling of the scene in Macduff's castle emphasises the family affection and the vulnerability of Lady Macduff and her son left defenceless by the absence of Macduff. Macduff's act of political bravery, in effect, sacrifices his innocent family to the brutality of tyranny. His bravery and honesty emerge in the long scene with Malcolm and in the end it is a poetic justice that Macduff should be the one to execute Macbeth. The final confrontation brings from Macbeth his only public confession of guilt when he says: 'my soul is too much charged/With blood of thine already.'

Duncan

Duncan is murdered in Act II, Scene 2 but in the eight scenes before that he has met Macbeth only once. Macbeth himself seems to avoid the King as much as possible so that it is Lady Macbeth who welcomes Duncan to Inverness and Macbeth does not even remain in the supper room with the king. Duncan is presented to us as a dignified, gentle and appreciative ruler. Macbeth is aware of Duncan's virtues and sees the enormity of his proposed murder of him. In the first Act, Scene 6 offers a picture of peace and trust in complete contrast to Scene 5 and the second half of Scene 7, and even Lady Macbeth sees a likeness to her own father in Duncan's sleeping face. Macbeth does not, cannot, describe the act of murdering Duncan; his hand seems to do a deed independently of his troubled mind. The treachery and deceit of Macbeth and Lady Macbeth are apparent in the ways they avoid calling the murder by its name but speak of 'business', 'provided for', 'deed' 'it', 'quell'. Macbeth's theatrical description of Duncan in Act II, Scene 3, lines 108–13 seems in its very ornateness to evade the horror, and the nastiness of the murder is most fully felt in Lady Macbeth's chilling question much later: 'Yet who would have thought the old man to have had so much blood in him?' (Act V, Scene 1, lines 38–9)

Malcolm

The flight of Malcolm on the murder of his father seems very sudden on the evidence given in the play. He is the chosen heir but he seems immediately to suspect that the fate of his father may come to him as well. In the early part of the play he is a dutiful attendant to his father. In his meeting with Macduff in Act IV, Scene 3, he reveals himself as a shrewd politician unwilling to commit himself till the evidence is clear. He tests Macduff's honesty at the same time as presenting himself as the very opposite of Macbeth. In the final act he is the instrument by which good government is to be restored to Scotland (with the help of England) and his deference to law and order is apparent not only in his final speech but, in the scenes leading up to the battle, in his willingness to bow to the knowledge of more experienced men. The connection between his style of speaking in his final speech and his father's manner in Act I, Scene 4 demonstrates the reassertion of virtue in the person of the king.

Meaning of the play

Macbeth is a play about the fall of man and his recovery from that fall. In Shakespeare's scheme of events the well-being of a country is at the mercy of the well-being of the ruler. The Porter and the Old Man and Ross may reflect on the disorder around them but they seem helpless to check such an upheaval:

> *Alas poor country,*
> *Almost afraid to know itself! It cannot*
> *Be called our mother, but our grave; where nothing*
> *But who knows nothing is once seen to smile;*
> *Where sighs and groans and shrieks that rent the air*
> *Are made, not marked; where violent sorrow seems*
> *A modern ecstasy.*
>
> (IV.3.164–170)

A new morality personified in Malcolm is needed to supplant evil. Macbeth's tyranny is the practise of devilish wickedness, his advisers are the 'instruments of darkness' and his unnatural rule can be opposed only with the help of the Christian God.

That, it seems, is the metaphysical framework erected by the structure and imagery of the play but the meaning of the work is not limited to such a theological interpretation. The play is, in many respects, like its Morality predecessors (see page 7), but Shakespeare's construction of his hero gives a new dimension to the struggle between good and evil. Macbeth is a nobleman, a good soldier, but these qualities are a mere surface in comparison with what we learn of his mind. He impresses us as an individual with his own complex and idiosyncratic way of seeing the world. We do not comprehend the reasons for his ambition but through his (and Shakespeare's) poetry we enter his hell with him. In the play the concept of man occurs in a number of places and for us the concept is humanised, individualised by Macbeth's experience. In Act I, Macbeth is fully aware of the danger his 'single state of man' is in and with the softness of his 'human kindness' he pronounces,

I dare do all that may become a man;
Who dares do more is none

By the end of the Act, however, he is taunted with his unmanliness by his wife, herself prepared to be dehumanised, to such an extent that he is prepared to 'bend up/Each corporal agent to this terrible deed' but when the deed is done he says 'To know the deed 'twere best not know myself'. The battle for his self-esteem is won and lost. He now comes to fear Banquo's 'being' (Act III, Scene 1, line 54) because of the latter's 'royalty of nature', and in his encounter with Banquo's ghost he becomes 'unmanned in folly', according to his wife. His courage can cope only with the physical; for any human attribute beyond the physical he feels fear or cynicism. The life of man is reduced to a procession of 'fools', a 'walking shadow', a performance of make-believe, the mouthing of an idiot. The humanity of Macduff's reaction to the news of his family's killing—'but I must also feel it as a man'—is a contrast that controls the conclusion of the play. We see the torment and the emptiness of Macbeth's life and we turn with relief to the dignity and humanity of Macduff and the order re-established by Malcolm. Macbeth, the usurper, the overreacher against these values, is exposed as a dwarfish thief in a giant's robe (See Act V, Scene 2, lines 20–2)

Macbeth's murder of King Duncan is not simply an act of political rebellion but, as he recognises in his soliloquy, Act I, Scene 7, lines 1–28, a violation of all the laws of hospitality, kinship and human decency. To Shakespeare's contemporaries the play must have offered a penetrating analysis of personal aspiration and political ambition. Even a good man, and the early reports in the play suggest that Macbeth had fine qualities, is pathetically vulnerable to the seductive and destructive possibilities of power.

Part 4

Hints for Study

Close reading

Background material and notes can give the reader some awareness of the general nature of the play, some sense of the climate of opinion in which the play was written, an indication of how highly others rate the play, but a full appreciation of the play must be based on a combination of the individual reader's close reading of the words before him and a sound sense of how the whole operates. Some general indication, helpful it is to be hoped, of the main ingredients which make up the whole was offered in Part 3, but many readers when confronted with Shakespeare's genius, feel abashed and hesitant at looking too closely at how he writes. A degree of humility is not a hindrance and a close examination or critical analysis is a difficult task requiring attention to detail, sensitivity to how the poetry works and some governing notion of the context in which the particular words and actions function.

The following analysis of one speech should offer some guidance as to what the reader may look for in a passage. The passage chosen is Macbeth's soliloquy occupying the second half of Act II, Scene 1. (In the editions of the play there is little disagreement about the line numbering in this scene and, in the interests of space, it has been assumed that the student has a text of his own to follow while reading the analysis.)

Form of the passage

The passage is in verse, apparently regular. There is only one interruption (the bell) and there is only one character present, Macbeth. The fact that the passage is a soliloquy is important because it means that what we are hearing is heard by no other character in the play and Macbeth can speak his mind frankly—he has nobody to deceive but himself. See section below on character revealed in the passage.

Context of the passage

Despite the customary act division there is no obvious break in time between the beginning of Act I, Scene 7 and the end of Act II, Scene

3. The soliloquy comes after the supper guests have retired to bed and immediately before the murder of Duncan. In Scene 7 we heard Macbeth wrestling with his conscience and finally being forced into preparedness by the forcefulness of his wife. Immediately after the murder Macbeth is almost helpless with anxiety and cannot pull his mind away from his experience in Duncan's bedroom. By Scene 3 he has partially recovered although his speech in lines 88–93 seems to hark back to Act I, Scene 7.

This placing of the soliloquy may seem over elaborate but no scene in a play operates independently of others around it and our awareness of this context gives added richness to the particular passage. Two examples are sufficient for the moment. At the end of Act I, Scene 7 Macbeth says, imitating the resolution and earlier words of his wife:

> *I am settled; and bend up*
> *Each corporal agent to this terrible feat.*
> *Away, and mock the time with fairest show:*
> *False face must hide what the false heart doth know.*

Some time later, he declines to discuss the Witches with Banquo. Now, in the soliloquy, we hear the thoughts of this 'settled' man who claims that he does not think of the Witches. His soliloquy is revealing in showing that Macbeth's control is not very firm. Left on his own, his mind imagines things and he cannot hold his imagination in check. The other example of the significance of the context looks forward to the following scene where his self-control has collapsed, and the incident of murdering Duncan is filled with noises so that he pleads, 'How is't with me when every noise appals me?' Now look again at the lines 56–60 of the soliloquy and beyond those to lines 16–25 of Act 1. Scene VII.

Character revealed in the passage

The soliloquy is Macbeth's final preparation of himself before the murder. What might we expect him to think about? The plan? The fear of discovery? What he must do as soon as the murder is committed? None of these things is spoken of directly by Macbeth; in fact, his thoughts seem to operate at a tangent to the deed ahead. He does not wonder about the difficulty of the task but he uses his imagination to shift his mind from the actual. Where does his imagined dagger come from? It seems to have a will of its own, 'Thou marshall'st me'. Macbeth pushes the dagger from his mind and replaces it with an atmosphere suitable to his intention and appropriate company (the figures of

Murder, the wolf and Tarquin). Only when his mind is so prepared is he ready to act, to act as an automaton. He has become an instrument hypnotized by himself to act when he receives the signal.

Style of the passage

(a) **Organisation:** There are four units in the soliloquy: lines 33–49, concerning the dagger; lines 49–56, voicing Macbeth's reverie on the world outside; lines 56–60, an invocation to the earth; lines 60–4, he moves into action. How does Macbeth's mind move from one unit to the next? The dagger arrives suddenly in the air and in line 48 Macbeth exerts his reason and attributes the appearance of the dagger to his preoccupation with the murder plan. The second unit is the result of Macbeth looking away from the dagger but his thoughts remain obstinately on the idea of the murder. The word 'Nature' should be a contrary force to his hallucination but it 'seems dead' and allows 'wicked dreams' to deceive sleeping man. Macbeth is still hallucinating. The ghost-like movement of Murder stalking his victim leads into the insistence on quietness in the third unit. The final unit is a break from the preceding lines. Here Macbeth repeats instructions to himself as if still unsure of what he is doing. Notice also that the threats he refers to have not taken place very solidly but he has filled in the time while awaiting the signal without losing his nerve. It is significant that Macbeth does not mention any person around him, not even his wife, and that he avoids naming his victim till the second last line.

(b) **Imagery:** This is not a heavily metaphorical piece like some that occur elsewhere in the play but there are some interesting choices of language. There is a move from sights to sounds in the soliloquy matching the furtiveness and tension of Macbeth. Human beings (but Macbeth really means himself) are strangely passive: the dagger offers its handle; it indicates directions; the eyes are made fools of; the 'bloody business' 'informs' and dreams 'abuse'; the bell 'invites' or 'summons'. Of course, the dagger itself with its suggestive movements and drops of blood is an image of Macbeth's troubled conscience which he cannot control, ('clutch') or be sure about. The 'heat-oppressed brain' which creates the elusive dagger is the same brain that is needed for the 'heat of deeds'. In the imagery of witchcraft and murder the concentration is on the sacrifice of innocence (the 'curtained sleep' and the pure Lucretia) by a secret and ruthless power. The only colours present in the soliloquy are those of darkness and blood.

(c) **Syntax and punctuation:** What is immediately noticeable is that the first and fourth units—see (a)—have different lengths of sentences from the middle units. Added together the first and fourth have about twelve sentences; the second and third have two or three. The first unit is marked by questions, exclamations, qualifications, repetitions, all suggesting uncertainty and jumpiness. The lines and sentences are subdivided so that, in reading them, one has a sense of Macbeth's unease. The final unit gives an impression of resolution but the resolution is so repeated and so tidily arranged that we suspect something glib and mechanical in it. In the middle units with their longer sentences we receive a sense of deliberation and suspense as if we have to hold our breath to read right through the sentences. There are more adjectives than in the other units and they give intensity to the thought. In the first and fourth units, also, there is a frequent mention of 'I', 'me', 'my', but in the middle units the word 'my' occurs twice only. This fits with the general words in these middle units: 'Nature', 'dreams', 'Witchcraft', 'Murder' against whom individual man seems helpless. The whole soliloquy is in the present tense except for 'was' in lines 42, 43 and 47. Macbeth seems unable to think of either the past or the future; he is rapt in the 'present horror'.

(d) **Verse:** The rhythm of the soliloquy coincides very closely with the syntax and we have a clear sound of Macbeth's doubts in the earlier part giving way to the measured strides of Murder. Notice the stress coming on the opening syllable of line 56, 'Moves like a ghost'; after the descriptive phrases, Murder approaches its victim firmly, inevitably. The stress falls, for the most part, on the final syllable of the line and as the quietness intensifies in the soliloquy this stress becomes more noticed until at the end Macbeth's mechanical resolution finds help in rhyming couplets. Notice also in the final five lines the repetition of vowel sounds particularly in 'threat', 'breath', 'bell', 'knell', 'Heaven', 'Hell' and 'he', 'heat' 'deeds', 'me', 'hear', 'thee', which give a complex crosspattern of sounds and words pulling the lines together and forcing the sense on our ears.

Passages to memorise

When answering a question on *Macbeth* or discussing the play it is necessary, in order to give your argument weight and substantiation, to refer in detail to passages in the play or, even better, to quote actual passages. Memorising pieces of Shakespeare is done not merely to support an argument; to hold lines in your head gives you the sound and feel of the play and makes the poetry live for you as no talking about the play can do. The following passages have been chosen with both uses, business and pleasure, in mind. Beside each passage are some notes of what is to be observed in the passage.

(a) Act I, Scene 3, lines 126–141 (Two truths ... what is not)

First revelation of Macbeth's mind; impact of Witches on Macbeth; confusion in Macbeth's thinking; imagination in Macbeth

(b) Act I, Scene 5, lines 13–28 (Glamis thou art ... crowned withall)

Lady Macbeth's analysis of Macbeth; contrast between Macbeth and his wife; her power over him

(c) Act I, Scene 5, lines 38–45 (Come, you spirits ... and it)

Lady Macbeth's determination; unnatural thoughts; invocation of evil

(d) Act I, Scene 7, lines 1–28 (If it were done ... the other)

Macbeth questions his plan; his scruples; his awareness of the consequences; his motivation; images of innocence

(e) Act II, Scene 2, lines 57–68 (Whence ... then)

Macbeth and Lady Macbeth's reactions to Duncan's murder; Macbeth's horror and conscience; Lady Macbeth's apparent calm; images of blood and water (compare (i)

(f) Act III, Scene 1, 47–56 (To be thus ... by Caesar)

Macbeth's fears of Banquo; his distrust of honesty and goodness; Banquo's character

(g) Act III, Scene 2, lines 4–22 (Naught's had ... ecstasy)

Lady Macbeth and Macbeth have doubts; they are no longer honest with each other; Lady Macbeth tries to comfort her husband; disorder of Macbeth's mind; compare Lady Macbeth with (i).

(h) Act III, Scene 4, lines 130–143 (There's not a one ... in deed)

Macbeth's insecurity; his dependence on the Witches; his new ruthlessness; no return; no room for thought; weakening of Lady Macbeth

(*i*) Act V, Scene 1, lines 34–43 (Out, damned spot . . . this starting)	Collapse of Lady Macbeth; her obsession with blood; compare her feminine quality with (*c*); compare also (*e*) and (*g*).
(*j*) Act V, Scene 5, lines 9–28 (I have . . . signifying nothing)	Hardness of Macbeth (compare (*a*) and (*e*)); emptiness of Macbeth; time has stopped; death of Lady Macbeth
(*k*) Act V, Scene 5, lines 42–52 (I pull in . . . our back)	The end in sight for Macbeth; the Witches are proved unreliable; Macbeth's determination to die fighting; compare (*b*).

Revision of the play

Exercises

1. Reread the whole play.
2. Write a summary of the plot allowing yourself three sentences for each act.
3. Ask someone to read out ten 2-line quotations from anywhere in the play. You have to identify the character speaking and the situation.
4. Describe from memory what happens in the final scene of each act.

Areas on which to concentrate

1. Character development (for example, Macbeth, Macduff) and comparisons (for example, Macbeth and Banquo; Macbeth and Lady Macbeth).
2. How Shakespeare creates suspense (for example, first two scenes of Act II), atmosphere (for example, Act I, Scene 3), antipathy (for example, Macbeth and Lady Macbeth's murder of Duncan) and sympathy (for example, Macduff's family in Act IV, Scene 2).
3. Use of the supernatural (for example, the Witches; ghosts; invocation of dark powers; prayers to God; Act II, Scene 4).
4. Particular speeches and scenes, their context and meaning (for example, Act I, Scene 3, lines 50–60; Act I, Scene 5, lines 58–68;

Act I, Scene 7, lines 47–59; Act III, Scene 1, lines 1–10; Act III, Scene 2, lines 45–55; Act IV, Scene 1, lines 143–155; Act IV, Scene 3, lines 164–173; Act V, Scene 1, lines 67–75; Act V, Scene 3, lines 19–28; Act V, Scene 6, lines 99–114; and Act I, Scene 1; Act I, Scene 6; Act II, Scene 4; the ghost scene in Act III, Scene 4; Act IV, Scene 2; Act V, Scene 1; Act V, Scene 5).

Essay and examination questions

Advice on how to answer a question:

(*i*) Read the question carefully and make sure that you understand what it is asking. It does not matter how much you know about other subjects or areas; you must answer this specific question. If the question asks '*How* does Shakespeare . . . ?' it is not enough to relate what happens. If you are asked to be critical, then you must try to assess the quality of what you are talking about. Always remember that *Macbeth* is a play and some sense of its dramatic manner (see section on structure, Part 3) should be apparent in your answer.

(*ii*) Prepare a plan of your answer. You plan should consist of: an introduction in which you examine the terms of the question and say what you propose to do; several main points in which you present or argue your case; and a conclusion in which you sum up what you have proved. Having such a plan concentrates your attention and helps you to organise what you know into a tidy and convincing pattern.

(*iii*) Choose quotations and incidents to illustrate and substantiate your main points. Without such actual evidence your argument may appear thin and arbitrary. Quotation also helps to give that sense of the play mentioned in the final sentence of (*i*) above.

An example of such a procedure: (this is a framework, not a whole answer)

QUESTION: Does Macbeth place less reliance on Lady Macbeth and more on the Witches as the play progresses? Give evidence to support your answer.

1. Understanding the question. This question asks for an answer, yes or no, and evidence is obviously needed to support your conclusion. Notice also that the situation you are asked to examine is not a static one but relates to the progression of the play.

2. Planning the answer.

Introduction. After the praise of him in Act I, Scene 2, Macbeth is characterised by fear and weakness much more than by bravery and strength: he needs to rely on someone. What is meant by saying someone places reliance on another? How is it measured?

(*a*) The other's advice is sought before he acts.

(*b*) The other's help is necessary for his success.

(*c*) The other's backing and trust are believed in.

Each of these three points needs to be looked at with Lady Macbeth and the Witches in mind. It is simpler to look at the characters separately. The comparison asked for in the question can be made in the conclusion.

3. Evidence.

Lady Macbeth

(*a*) Macbeth seldom directly asks his wife's opinion on anything. His letter in Act I, Scene 5 suggests that they have earlier discussed the possibility of his becoming king. In the scene she gives her advice and when he wavers (line 69) she so forces her opinion on Macbeth that he declares at the end 'I am settled'. Similarly in Scene 7.

Macbeth does not consult his wife before the murders of Banquo and Macduff's family.

(*b*) The murder of Duncan seems inconceivable without Lady Macbeth. The force of her character in this affair helps Macbeth to act at all and rescues him from his own weakness. Similarly in Act III, Scenes 2 and 4 when she pushes him on and defends him against collapse.

(*c*) There is an affection and loyalty between Macbeth and his wife. He has evidence that he can expect her support but he does not appear to use it after Act III, Scene 4.

The Witches

(*a*) Macbeth asks the Witches to speak in Act I and tell him more. In Act III, Scene 4 he declares to his wife that he intends to consult the Witches.

In Act IV he demands that they answer his questions.

(*b*) The Witches give no practical help to Macbeth.

(*c*) His invocation of powers of darkness before each murder gives him some confidence of success.

After his visit in Act IV, Scene 1 Macbeth feels that the words of the Witches give him protection but he does not accept what they show for Banquo's heirs.

When Birnam Wood approaches he begins to 'doubt the equivocation of the fiend/That lies like truth' and in the final scene when on hearing the truth about Macduff's birth he says

> *And be these juggling friends no more believed*
> *That palter us in a double sense,*
> *That keep the word of promise to our ear*
> *And break it to our hope.*

4. Conclusion

Macbeth's relationship with, and reliance on, his wife and the Witches are of different sorts. Certainly in Acts IV and V his wife has no prominence and in Act III he acts on his own initiative. In Act V the promises of the Witches sustain him but in the end he dies, disillusioned and on his own. The general answer is a qualified yes.

What to avoid

(Unless you are specifically asked to do so)
Do not tell everything you know about the play or author.
Do not merely relate the plot.
Do not copy out all the quotations you have memorised just to show that you know them.

Questions

These questions are designed to give some indication of the kind of questions usually asked about *Macbeth* and to encourage you to explore the play more deeply for yourself.

(1) Compare and contrast Macbeth and Lady Macbeth in the first two Acts of the play.

(2) Who or what are the Witches and what effect do they have on Macbeth?

(3) What does Macduff contribute to the play?

(4) Discuss the dramatic importance of the first two scenes of the play.

(5) How does Lady Macbeth's sleep-walking scene relate to earlier parts of the play?

(6) Attempt to determine how and when the idea of murdering Duncan emerges in Macbeth's mind.

(7) In what ways is Banquo an important character?

(8) Discuss the relationship between Macbeth and his wife during the play.

(9) Analyse Macbeth's state of mind in the first two scenes of Act II.

(10) Discuss Shakespeare's presentation of Duncan *or* Malcolm.

(11) Compare Macbeth and Banquo up to the murder of Duncan.

(12) Why does Macbeth kill Banquo?

(13) Do you consider the supper scene (Act III, Scene 4) to be the turning-point of Macbeth's career?

(14) Is Macbeth loathsome or heroic or a mixture of the two in the final Act of the play?

(15) How would you show that the play is not just about Macbeth as an individual?

Part 5

Suggestions for further reading

The text

The best modern editions of the play
Macbeth, edited by Kenneth Muir, (The New Arden Shakespeare)
Methuen, London, 1951.
Macbeth, edited by J. Dover Wilson, (The New Cambridge Shakespeare) Cambridge University Press, Cambridge, 1947.
Macbeth, edited by G.K. Hunter, (The New Penguin Shakespeare)
Penguin Books, Harmondsworth, 1967.
Macbeth, edited by Sylvan Barnett, (The Signet Classic Shakespeare)
New English Library, London, 1963.
Macbeth, edited by Bernard Lott, (New Swan Shakespeare,) Longman,
London, 1978.
All references in this book are to the New Penguin Shakespeare edition.

Books on Shakespeare and *Macbeth*

MUIR, KENNETH and SCHOENBAUM, S. (ED.): *A New Companion to Shakespeare Studies*, Cambridge University Press, Cambridge, 1971. This contains useful essays on Shakespeare's background and subjects related to his work.

LERNER, LAURENCE (ED.): *Shakespeare's Tragedies, An Anthology of Modern Criticism*, Penguin Books, Harmondsworth, 1968. This contains a variety of views on *Macbeth* and the general question of tragedy.

WAIN, JOHN (ED.): *Shakespeare Macbeth, A Selection of Critical Essays*, Macmillan Casebook Series, Macmillan, London, 1968. This includes well-chosen pieces ranging from Dr. Johnson and Coleridge to the most significant modern essays by such critics as Bradley, Freud, Wilson Knight and Cleanth Brooks.

HAWKES, TERENCE (ED.): *Twentieth Century Interpretations of Macbeth*, Prentice-Hall, New Jersey, 1977. This includes recent views of the play.

The author of these notes

Alasdair D.F. Macrae was educated at the University of Edinburgh. He taught for a short time in secondary schools before taking up a lectureship in the University of Khartoum, Republic of the Sudan. Since 1969 he has been a lecturer in English Studies at the University of Stirling. The author of other York Notes, he is at present completing studies of the poetry of Shelley and Edwin Muir.

The first 100 titles

ACHEBE	*Arrow of God* *Things Fall Apart*
JANE AUSTEN	*Northanger Abbey* *Pride and Prejudice* *Sense and Sensibility*
ROBERT BOLT	*A Man For All Seasons*
CHARLOTTE BRONTË	*Jane Eyre*
EMILY BRONTË	*Wuthering Heights*
ALBERT CAMUS	*L'Etranger (The Stranger)*
GEOFFREY CHAUCER	*Prologue to the Canterbury Tales* *The Franklin's Tale* *The Knight's Tale* *The Nun's Priest's Tale* *The Pardoner's Tale*
SIR ARTHUR CONAN DOYLE	*The Hound of the Baskervilles*
JOSEPH CONRAD	*Nostromo*
DANIEL DEFOE	*Robinson Crusoe*
CHARLES DICKENS	*David Copperfield* *Great Expectations*
GEORGE ELIOT	*Adam Bede* *Silas Marner* *The Mill on the Floss*
T.S. ELIOT	*The Waste Land*
WILLIAM FAULKNER	*As I Lay Dying*
F. SCOTT FITZGERALD	*The Great Gatsby*
E.M. FORSTER	*A Passage to India*
ATHOL FUGARD	*Selected Plays*
MRS GASKELL	*North and South*

WILLIAM GOLDING	*Lord of the Flies*
OLIVER GOLDSMITH	*The Vicar of Wakefield*
THOMAS HARDY	*Jude the Obscure* *Tess of the D'Urbervilles* *The Mayor of Casterbridge* *The Return of the Native* *The Trumpet Major*
L.P. HARTLEY	*The Go-Between*
ERNEST HEMINGWAY	*For Whom the Bell Tolls* *The Old Man and the Sea*
ANTHONY HOPE	*The Prisoner of Zenda*
RICHARD HUGHES	*A High Wind in Jamaica*
THOMAS HUGHES	*Tom Brown's Schooldays*
HENRIK IBSEN	*A Doll's House*
HENRY JAMES	*The Turn of the Screw*
BEN JONSON	*The Alchemist* *Volpone*
D.H. LAWRENCE	*Sons and Lovers* *The Rainbow*
HARPER LEE	*To Kill a Mocking-Bird*
SOMERSET MAUGHAM	*Selected Short Stories*
HERMAN MELVILLE	*Billy Budd* *Moby Dick*
ARTHUR MILLER	*Death of a Salesman* *The Crucible*
JOHN MILTON	*Paradise Lost I & II*
SEAN O'CASEY	*Juno and the Paycock*
GEORGE ORWELL	*Animal Farm* *1984*
JOHN OSBORNE	*Look Back in Anger*
HAROLD PINTER	*The Birthday Party*
J.D. SALINGER	*The Catcher in the Rye*
SIR WALTER SCOTT	*Ivanhoe* *Quentin Durward*

WILLIAM SHAKESPEARE	*A Midsummer Night's Dream*
	Antony and Cleopatra
	Coriolanus
	Cymbeline
	Hamlet
	Henry IV Part I
	Henry V
	Julius Caesar
	King Lear
	Macbeth
	Much Ado About Nothing
	Othello
	Richard II
	Romeo and Juliet
	The Merchant of Venice
	The Tempest
	The Winter's Tale
	Troilus and Cressida
	Twelfth Night
GEORGE BERNARD SHAW	*Androcles and the Lion*
	Arms and the Man
	Caesar and Cleopatra
	Pygmalion
RICHARD BRINSLEY SHERIDAN	*The School for Scandal*
JOHN STEINBECK	*Of Mice and Men*
	The Grapes of Wrath
	The Pearl
ROBERT LOUIS STEVENSON	*Kidnapped*
	Treasure Island
JONATHAN SWIFT	*Gulliver's Travels*
W.M. THACKERAY	*Vanity Fair*
MARK TWAIN	*Huckleberry Finn*
	Tom Sawyer
VOLTAIRE	*Candide*
H.G. WELLS	*The History of Mr. Polly*
	The Invisible Man
	The War of the Worlds
OSCAR WILDE	*The Importance of Being Earnest*